G   UTES
NORTHWEST ENGLAND

DORIAN SPEAKMAN
& COLIN SPEAKMAN

DIAL HOUSE

First published 2001

ISBN 0 7110 2780 3

Published by Dial House

an imprint of Ian Allan Publishing Ltd,
Hersham, Surrey KT12 4RG.
Printed by Ian Allan Printing Ltd,
Hersham, Surrey KT12 4RG.

Code: 0105/D

Cover: Brampton Market Hall and (*inset*)
cyclist near Milburn

Title page:
The Coal Road.

This page:
Descending on a lane
towards Ulverston.

GREAT CYCLE ROUTES IN NORTHWEST ENGLAND

This book is designed to introduce the cyclist to two of the most rewarding counties in England for cyclists — Cumbria and Lancashire. Unlike flatter parts of the country, such as East Anglia, Cheshire or East Yorkshire, both are fairly hilly and even, in places, mountainous areas. Nevertheless, they offer some superb cycling opportunities, not just around the flatter if somewhat narrow coastal plains, but further inland in areas like the Eden Valley in eastern Cumbria which, because of their relative lack of traffic, are amongst the most delightful for the cyclist in northwest England.

The book assumes that the reader has some experience of cycling but would like a day on quiet roads enjoying the best countryside and many interesting attractions that the two counties have to offer. The routes described range from a pleasant short afternoon's ride to a full day's excursion. They are meant for the average cyclist who is out to enjoy a pleasant ride rather than cover long distances. Wherever possible busy main roads are avoided, although in the more heavily populated or popular tourist areas of both counties some short sections of busy roads are inevitable if you want to enjoy the best rides.

This book is not designed for the mountain biker. The routes are almost entirely on tarmac, using minor roads and back lanes wherever possible. However, short sections of off-road bridleway have been suggested to provide a short cut or to avoid long, unpleasant detours along heavily trafficked main roads. There are also some sections of cycleway used which are unsurfaced or covered only with crushed stones or ash. An indication of the surfaces to be encountered is therefore given at the beginning of every ride.

The ideal cycle for these routes is either a touring machine or one of the new 'hybrids', sometimes known as 'comfort all-terrain' bikes, which with heavier tyres and more solid construction can cope with everything in this book quite easily whilst still giving the greater comfort and speed of a touring bike. On the other hand, as distances are generally not great on these routes, a mountain bike is perfectly acceptable; such a machine was in fact used for researching several of these routes.

To help reduce the need to cope with heavy traffic, the rides avoid concentrated urban areas as much as possible. Instead, the train is used to get the cyclist away from the maze of urban streets and highways and straight out into the quieter countryside. Many rides are linear in nature, enabling you to get the most from a ride out and to relax on the train for the return trip.

This is also a book, therefore, which will have special value for non-car-owning cyclists. Too many cycle guides are really nothing more than car-bike rides, starting from car parks totally inaccessible without your own vehicle. For this reason, each ride in this book starts from a railway station, usually where there is a good rail service — in most cases Sundays included. Car drivers are, however, most certainly not excluded, and are advised as to the best place to park — usually in the station car park if a train has to be used

Below:
Ullswater from Waterfoot.

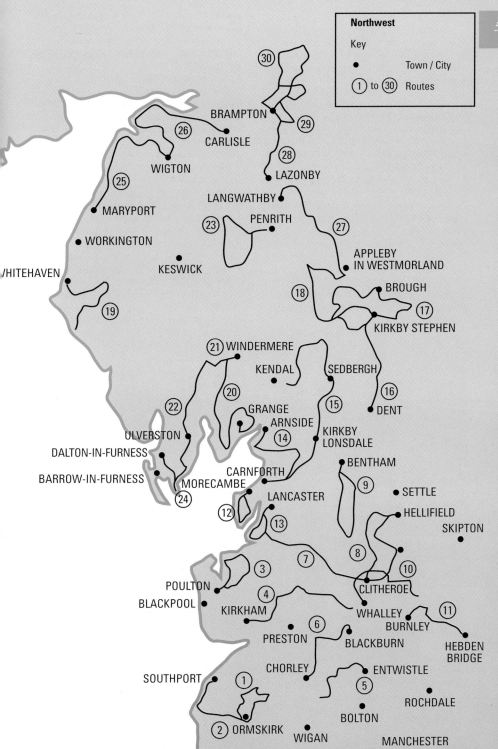

Northwest

Key

● Town / City

① to ㉚   Routes

㉚

BRAMPTON

㉖

CARLISLE

㉙

WIGTON

㉕

㉘

LAZONBY

MARYPORT

LANGWATHBY

㉓ PENRITH

㉗

● WORKINGTON

APPLEBY
IN WESTMORLAND

WHITEHAVEN

KESWICK

⑱ BROUGH

㉔ ⑰
KIRKBY STEPHEN

⑲

㉑ WINDERMERE

KENDAL

SEDBERGH

⑳

⑯

㉒

GRANGE

⑮ DENT

ULVERSTON

ARNSIDE

⑭

KIRKBY
LONSDALE

DALTON-IN-FURNESS

BENTHAM

BARROW-IN-FURNESS

CARNFORTH

⑨

MORECAMBE

SETTLE

㉔

LANCASTER

HELLIFIELD

⑫

SKIPTON

⑬

⑧

⑩

⑦

③

CLITHEROE

POULTON

④

⑪

BLACKPOOL

KIRKHAM

WHALLEY

BURNLEY

⑥

HEBDEN
BRIDGE

PRESTON

BLACKBURN

CHORLEY

ENTWISTLE

SOUTHPORT

①

⑤

ROCHDALE

② ORMSKIRK

BOLTON

WIGAN

MANCHESTER

— to take advantage of the railway facility. It is important to remember that using the train rather than driving long distances for all or part of a journey reduces congestion and pollution in the environment, as well as being more relaxing at the end of a ride. Some rail routes, such as the awe-inspiring Settle-Carlisle line or the beautiful Furness and West Cumbria lines, are worth a trip in their own right, being part of the pleasure of a day out.

With so much variety in landscape, population density and tourist activity, the cyclist is likely to come across widely differing traffic conditions in Lancashire and Cumbria. We have tried to keep to quiet back lanes wherever possible, though many B roads and even some A roads in Cumbria are quiet enough to make cycling very enjoyable. Many of the routes have been designed to link up with others in this book, so that with a bit of imagination two or more rides can be combined for a weekend visit or a longer stay. This makes better use of the cost and time of a car or rail journey from home. With many bed-and-breakfast establishments and youth hostels available, this book can therefore be used to plan an excellent long weekend or short mid-week break in some of England's loveliest and least known cycling country. The routes are simply a selection of what is on offer — hopefully they will inspire the reader to further explore England's northwestern counties armed with a bike, a map and a rail timetable!

Finally, please bear in mind that, although all the routes and connecting rail services have been thoroughly researched and tested by the authors, timetables, signing and even road junctions can change, new cycle tracks can appear, and so on.

THE LANDSCAPE

Lancashire has a quite amazing variety of scenery within its boundaries. To the south are the heavily industrialised and urbanised regions surrounding Manchester, Liverpool, Preston and the former East Lancashire cotton towns of Blackburn and Burnley. These areas, with their housing estates, motorways and heavy traffic, are in direct contrast to the open, brown moors, reservoirs and river valleys of the West and South Pennines and the Forest of Bowland. The West Lancashire Plain is fertile, mostly

Lakeside & Haverthwaite Railway.
Barry Stacey/Cumbria Tourist Board

flat, farmland, which narrows increasingly as the Pennines approach the coast near Lancaster. There is some delightful cycling here but because of high population densities it is rarely possible to escape at least some traffic even in quiet back roads. In the middle of Lancashire the Ribble Valley cuts a course from the Yorkshire Dales down through Bowland and Pendle and provides excellent, if undulating, cycling country within easy reach of the towns of Blackburn and Preston.

North of Morecambe Bay lies Cumbria, with the Lake District mountains lying at the heart of the county. The Lake District is not easy cycling country because of the severe gradients and the heavy tourist traffic in the central areas. However, it is fringed by a spectacular coastline to the south and west, including Furness and West Cumbria, which are relatively little known and offer some excellent cycling opportunities, as do the rolling hills and limestone scars to the east where the Lake District meets the Pennines. Further east, where the high North Pennines escarpments overlook the tranquil Eden Valley, with its characteristic red sandstone and network of virtually traffic-free lanes, there is some superb cycling country. Further north still, the region is crossed by Hadrian's Wall which runs from the coast of the Solway Firth inland up the Irthing Valley to Northumberland. Beyond the Wall is rough hill country, once home to the Reivers, the fearsome raiders of the Scottish borderlands. As in the Eden Valley, the network of quiet lanes with relatively little traffic makes this cycling country par excellence.

Apart from the very narrow coastal strip, therefore, you cannot escape the hills, and there are some pretty brutish gradients in the Bowland and Pennine foothills, with their steep tributary valleys. The answer is to have plenty of gears available, to take your time (and not be ashamed of walking up the steepest gradients) and to enjoy the landscape and some of the many fascinating heritage attractions — country houses, castles, ancient churches and nature reserves — that these routes take you past. The suggested times for each route are deliberately on the generous side to include meal stops — there are plenty of cafés and pubs available — but we suggest that you add time to visit some of the places en route.

THE NATIONAL CYCLE NETWORK
Sustrans, the national cycling charity, has been creating a National Cycle Network throughout Britain. The National Cycle Network aims to achieve a high-quality network of safe and attractive routes on a combination of totally traffic-free paths, protected sections of cycle track on minor roads, and quiet back roads and byways. The network will be completed by 2005, but already a good part of it is in place and sections are used on certain routes in this book.

Details of the National Cycle Network and other major cycle routes across Cumbria and Lancashire are given on page 108

CYCLE CARRIAGE ON TRAINS
The carriage of bikes on trains in the northwest of England is generally possible at all times except during morning rush hours into the main towns and cities, at certain other peak times such as summer Saturday mornings into popular resorts such as Blackpool and Windermere, and on busy Manchester Airport services where luggage space can be at a premium.

However, since privatisation each different train operating company has its own rules for carrying cycles on its train services. At the time of writing, most local

Above:
Signposts at a junction near Kirkbride, with the Lakeland fells behind.

services in Lancashire and Cumbria are operated by First North Western. Cycles are carried free of charge on all First North Western services at the discretion of the conductor, but space is generally limited to two cycles per train on a 'first come, first served' basis. Groups of three or more are therefore advised to enquire about availability on particular services. Reservations are also recommended on all services to or from Manchester Airport at peak times. For general enquiries ring 0870 241 2305 and for cycle reservation on specific services ring 0845 604 0231.

A number of important cross-country services through Lancashire and Cumbria are operated by Northern Spirit, including Transpennine Express services between West Yorkshire, Burnley, Blackburn, Preston and Blackpool, services along the Tyne Valley line serving Brampton and Carlisle, and all services along the Settle-Carlisle line, except for summer Sunday Dales Rail services from Preston and Blackburn which are operated by First North Western.

Most Northern Spirit services have space for at least two cycles. On Transpennine Express and Leeds-Settle-Carlisle services reservations are recommended at busy times, especially summer Saturdays, and are free to customers, otherwise space is allocated on a 'first come, first served' basis. The telephone number for further information is 0870 602 3322.

Merseyrail operates the electrified local rail services from Liverpool to Southport and Ormskirk. Cycles are carried free of charge on all services at any time, space permitting.

Along the West Coast main line between Manchester/Wigan, Preston, Lancaster, Penrith and Carlisle InterCity services are operated by Virgin Trains. West Coast and Cross Country services carry up to four cycles per train (certain Cross Country services take up to 10), at a charge of £3

per single journey, but advance booking is recommended especially at busy times. The cycle ticket has to be purchased at the same time as the rail ticket, but can be also purchased by telephone with a credit card: telephone 08457 222 333.

ACCESS TO STATIONS
This book assumes that there is relatively easy bike access to your local railway station, although bear in mind that at many stations platform access is via steps — so look out for lifts or be prepared to carry your bike. Carlisle and Lancaster councils have produced cycling maps which you can get at local book stores or else from the city councils' cycling departments. If you find that cycle access to your station is not good enough, then please write a letter to the council's highways department and contact your local cycling group — change is possible but only if you act!

USING YOUR CAR
Although this book aims to encourage the use of the cycle and train as much as possible, you may well find that you have to use the car to transport your bike(s) to the railway station.

A popular method is to use a back carrier which is fitted to the rear of the car using a combination of straps, clips and adjustable angles. This type of rack usually carries two bikes. Another method of carrying bikes on the outside of the car is to use a specially designed roofrack. Some are designed to carry the bikes upside

Left:
Gleaston Castle.

Right:
The village green and café at Slaidburn.

down and others the right way up. The advantage of this system is that it does not restrict the driver's rear view, but it can affect the car's wind resistance and you need to be pretty strong to lift your bike on to the roof, especially if it is a heavy mountain bike.

Another option, used by some motorists, is to carry the bikes in the back of an estate car or larger hatchback. Quick-release wheels means that most bikes will fit into the back of a car, though it may restrict the number of passengers you can carry with you.

PRACTICAL POINTS
Planning Your Trip
If you are relatively new to cycling, or have not cycled much apart from very short trips, make a note of the terrain and distance. It is best to start on some of the easier, flatter routes and build yourself up gradually.

The selection of rides is designed to make maximum use of back roads where the traffic is light, but does assume that you (and any children accompanying you) have some experience of road traffic. In some routes short sections of often very busy main roads have had to be used; these are mentioned in the text.

Below: Panniers, ideal for transporting everything the keen cyclist needs for a lengthy ride. *Simon Joslin*

What to Take — Checklist
- Cycle repair kit (including a spare inner tube)
- Pump
- Waterproofs
- Water bottle
- Suntan cream (essential on a sunny day; it is amazing how quickly legs, arms and necks can burn)
- Insect repellent (useful if cycling through a forest in summer, when midges and mosquitoes can be rampant!)
- Food, either snack or packed lunch
- Lock
- Money
- Hand wipes (great for getting oil off your hands after an unexpected repair)
- Lights/reflective belt (essential if there is the remotest chance you will be out after dusk)
- Map/guidebook
- Hat/gloves

Always take an emergency set of tools, so that you can repair a puncture or make adjustments to your bike while on the road. This would include: pump, inner tube, Allen keys, adjustable spanner, screwdriver, tyre levers (at least two), chain link remover, and puncture repair kit.

In hot weather it is advisable to take at least 1 litre of water, and to buy drinks en route. Whilst you can always buy food on the trip, also have some sandwiches and energy food like flapjacks to keep you going.

Above: Frame pouch and saddlebag, handy
for shorter trips. *Simon Joslin*

Right: Emergency repairs! *Dave Williamson*

Carrying the Essentials

The anticipated weather for the day and the
length of time you expect to be out will
influence how much you will want to carry
with you on your bike. The easiest way to
carry things is with panniers which attach
to a metal carrier on the rear of the bike.
Alternatively, for short trips in good
weather, a saddle bag which can be
attached to the rear of a saddle or a frame
pouch may be enough for tools and small
items of food. Whenever possible avoid
carrying things on your back on the bike
— a rucksack can not only be a strain on
the back, but can throw you off balance,
perhaps with disastrous effect.

Preparation

Before you leave home check the following
on your bike:

■ Brakes: Check that the front and back
brakes are working. Also check that the
cables and brake blocks are not worn,
otherwise they will require replacement.

■ Tyres: Check that the tyres are pumped
up hard. Also check the tread is not
worn or the valves damaged, otherwise
the tyre or inner tube may need
replacing. There is now a fluid available
that is pumped into inner tubes (so far
available only for mountain bike inner
tubes) that can counter punctures.
Otherwise it is possible to get inner
tubes made from tougher material.

■ Chain: Check that it is well oiled
and not slack.

■ Saddle: Check that it is the right height
so that you can touch the ground with
your toes when sitting in the saddle, but
that it is high enough to have your legs
almost straight when pedalling. This is
particularly important for children's
bikes.

■ Gears: Check these are working. If
there are problems, other than minor
adjustments, they will usually require
the attention of a bike shop.

Above: Checking gear operation and chain.
Simon Joslin

Above: Check the brakes, wheels and spokes.
Simon Joslin

- Wheels: Check for broken spokes or buckled wheels. If damaged, the bike will need to go to a shop for repair.

- Lights: Check they are working (back and front) and not in need of a new battery or bulb.

- Bell: Be considerate to other users on cyclepaths, and use the bell to warn walkers when you approach. Have one fitted — and use it.

Make sure you know how to fix a puncture: the ubiquitous broken glass of British urban areas is a curse for today's cyclist. Most puncture repair kits have clear instructions on the back of the box to help — but you might practise removing and replacing a tyre and inner tube before you have to do it in the pouring rain on a remote hillside.

Lock Up!
Bicycle thefts are on the increase, even in rural areas, so even if you are intending to stop for only a short time, it is advisable to lock your bike up, if only to avoid being stranded in a remote location! Always try to lock your bike to something, preferably a solid object such as a lamp post or fence. The best type of lock to use is a reinforced black steel U-lock, which requires special equipment to cut open without a key. Other types of lock are easily removed by enterprising thieves using bolt cutters. It is also advisable to have a record of your frame identity number, so that in the event of your bike being stolen, you have some chance of recovering it.

Clothing and Footwear
Spare clothing in layers is useful in case the weather turns for the worse, or if during the return journey the evening is cool. You do not have to go to the expense of buying designer cycle wear — but it is suggested that you wear natural fibres that allow the skin to breathe. A foldable, lightweight waterproof is useful, too. However, it is advisable to keep the weight down, as you may well have to climb steps while carrying your bike over a footbridge at a station.

Stretchable trousers or leggings which are tight at the leg are ideal for cycling. Avoid baggy tracksuits which can easily be caught in the chain, or thick non-stretch material like denim which can get very uncomfortable on a longer ride when the seams can rub the inside of your leg. The best all-route solution, for those intending to do a lot of cycling, is a pair of padded cycling shorts, which will provide excellent protection against saddle-sore behinds. For footwear, any reasonably hard-wearing flat-soled shoe or trainer is suitable.

If you are riding in dusky or dark conditions it is a good idea to be wearing light or reflective clothing to make yourself more visible.

A well-fitted bike helmet is strongly advised for any cycling trip, as the head is the most crucial area of the body to protect. A helmet also has the advantage of keeping off some of the rain in wet weather, or reducing the effects of a cold headwind!

Above:
Lightweight Cycle helmet, essential equipment
Simon Joslin

The Lancaster Canal basin, Glasson Dock.

MARTIN MERE AND RUFFORD OLD HALL: TOWN GREEN (AUGHTON) TO RUFFORD

This gentle ride across the West Lancashire Plain is the ideal first ride in this book. It runs from Clieves Hill near Ormskirk, following the meanderings of the Leeds-Liverpool Canal as it crosses the plain. The highlight of the ride is Martin Mere, a remnant of a much larger lake which over the centuries has been drained to become rich vegetable-producing farmland. Martin Mere is the home of the Wildfowl and Wetlands Trust and you should allow yourself time to enjoy its extraordinary birdlife, before continuing by Mere Sands Wood Nature Reserve to the village of Rufford, rich in heritage interest.

BACKGROUND AND PLACES OF INTEREST:

West Lancashire Plain

The lush green West Lancashire countryside between the Ribble and the Mersey once contained much peaty marshland or moss. When drained (the many drainage channels or dykes are key features of the landscape), the land produced some of the richest agricultural soils in England, famed for the growing of potatoes, vegetables and for market gardening. It is also

Below: On the route near Scarisbrick

excellent cycling country, with a network of quiet lanes with few gradients, and many features of heritage interest, some of which are explored on this ride.

Martin Mere

Martin Mere is a wetland sanctuary of international importance where you can see a huge variety of both common and exotic ducks and geese. Sited by Martin Mere, the centre has a complex of ponds that is home to wetland birds from all over the world. There are hides with views over the main lake, and a children's play area. There is also a visitor centre, with a variety of souvenirs and guidebooks, a gallery with paintings and prints of birds and a popular café. The centre, which is open daily, is owned and managed by the Wildfowl and Wetlands Trust, and the entrance charge helps to fund the trust's conservation work.

Mere Sands Wood Nature Reserve

This nature reserve owned by the Lancashire Trust for Nature Conservation is situated in a former sandstone quarry, now a series of shallow lakes. It is rich in geological interest, with areas of heathland and marsh creating a habitat with a wide variety of birdlife to be enjoyed from well-screened hides, and a series of walking trails through the woods. Access is free on weekdays but on Sundays the reserve is open only to LTNC members.

Rufford

Rufford village has pretty white-walled houses, a fine Victorian Gothic church noted for its stained glass windows and a small park or green which every May Day bank holiday hosts a medieval fair to celebrate the granting of its market and fair charter in the 12th century.

Rufford Old Hall

Reputed to be one of the finest 15th century buildings in the north, this splendid late medieval half-timbered hall, ancestral home of the Hesketh family, is now owned and managed by the National Trust. One story has it that William Shakespeare as a young actor performed there with his colleagues for the then owner Sir Thomas Hesketh. The hall itself is remarkable for its ornate screen and hammerbeam roof and its fine collections of 17th century oak furniture and 16th century arms and armour and tapestries. Outside there are extensive gardens, as well as a picnic site and a restaurant. Rufford Old Hall is open daily except Thursdays and Fridays (although it is open on these days in August). Cycle parking is available.

Starting Point: Town Green railway station. Merseyrail trains every 15min weekdays, every 30min Sundays from Liverpool Central and Ormskirk. Trains from Preston every 90min connect with Liverpool trains at Ormskirk. Motorists should park at Town Green (or at Ormskirk, and take the train out to Town Green) and return by train from Rufford.

Finishing/Return Point: Rufford. Trains run every 90min to Preston and Ormskirk. Ormskirk trains connect with Merseyrail trains to Town Green and Liverpool Central. Note there is no Sunday service between Ormskirk and Rufford. Alternatively, Martin Mere and Rufford can be reached from Burscough Bridge station which has a more frequent train service between Manchester, Wigan and Southport (for Liverpool), including an hourly Sunday service. Burscough Bridge station lies 3km (2 miles) east of Martin Mere via back roads, whilst Rufford is 4km (3 miles) to the north. There is also a limited weekday service direct from New Lane station to Southport and Manchester.

Distance: 24km (15 miles).

Time: $2^1/_2$ hr plus adequate time to visit Martin Mere and Rufford Old Hall.

Map: OS Landranger 108: Liverpool & Surrounding Area.

Surfaces and Gradients: Virtually flat — and even a short downhill section.

Traffic Conditions: Mainly quiet lanes, but some busy main road crossings where care is required.

Facilities: Cafés: Martin Mere Wildfowl Centre, Rufford Old Hall.
Pubs: Pinfold, Heaton's Bridge, New Lane, Rufford.
Shops: Town Green (Aughton), Rufford.
WCs: Martin Mere, Rufford Old Hall.

ROUTE INSTRUCTIONS:
From Town Green station turn left on to Town Green Lane then turn right on to Winifred Lane. Follow Winifred Lane up to the A59 roundabout and go straight ahead on to the road signed for Formby. At the next roundabout turn left (signed for Formby) then take the next right, Fir Tree Lane. Follow this lane along the ridge of Clieves Hill until it drops down into the plain and ends at a T-junction.

Turn right and follow the road to the next junction. Turn right, then at the next junction turn left on to North Moor Lane. Follow this lane until just before the narrow bridge and turn right on to Small Lane.

Turn right at the next junction and follow the lane as far as the A570. Cross straight over (with care as the view is restricted), taking the road ahead which is slightly to the right. Follow this lane as far as Heaton's Bridge, and turn left on to the B5242. Cross over the Leeds-Liverpool Canal and take the next turn right.

At the next junction go right once again (signed Burscough) and continue along this lane as it follows the canal. At the next junction turn left this time and follow the road over the level crossing by New Lane station. At the T-junction turn left on to Fish Lane. Martin Mere is about 300m along this road.

From Martin Mere continue along in the same direction and take the next right. Follow this narrow lane until it ends at a T-junction then turn left up to the B5246. Turn right and continue along this road into Rufford, passing Mere Sands Wood Nature Reserve on the right. In Rufford turn left on to the A59. The first road on the right past Rufford Church (take care turning as traffic is usually busy) leads to Rufford station, whilst Rufford Old Hall entrance is a few hundred metres further north; the entrance is directly off the A59 on the right.

ROUTE 1
MARTIN MERE
TOWN GREEN (AUGHTON) TO RUFFORD

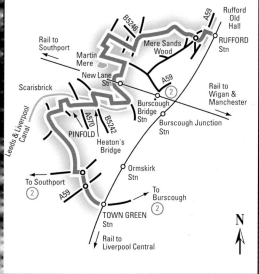

ACROSS THE WEST LANCASHIRE PLAIN: SOUTHPORT TO BURSCOUGH

A ride from the popular resort of Southport alongside the sand dunes before heading inland to the market gardening country of the West Lancashire coastal plain. A gentle climb near Ormskirk offers fine views across to Liverpool and towards the Pennines. The final part of the ride runs along twisting lanes and rolling fields before dropping down to the open countryside traversed by canals and railways.

BACKGROUND AND PLACES OF INTEREST:

Southport

One of Lancashire's premier seaside resorts, Southport combines elegance, charm and good old-fashioned seaside ebullience. There is a lot of sand although it does not really have a good beach in terms of seabathing. There are fine views across the Ribble estuary, extensive gardens and very good visitor facilities. Crossens Marsh just to the north of the town beyond the foreshore has been described as a 'birdwatchers' dream' because of the wide variety of birdlife to be seen on the salt marshes.

Ainsdale National Nature Reserve

The coastline below Southport through Ainsdale to Formby Point, with its dunes and pines, is amongst the most important in Britain for coastal and dune wildlife, with a diverse flora and nationally rare species such as the sand lizard, great crested newt, natterjack toad and red squirrel. There are marked paths into the reserves easily reached from this ride.

Leeds-Liverpool Canal and Burscough

The 203km (127-mile) Leeds-Liverpool Canal crosses the coastal plain on its route to the coalfields of Wigan, being opened to Wigan as early as 1774. On the way it goes through the canalside village of Burscough Bridge, where there is still a canal maintenance yard. Before the railway was built to Southport, passenger packet boats ran between Liverpool and Wigan, with a special horse-drawn road carriage service taking passengers on to the newly established seaside resort of Southport. By 1821 Southport had grown sufficiently in importance to justify a Manchester-Scarisbrick packet-boat service. The 11km-long (7-mile) Rufford branch of the canal, opened in 1781, leaves the main Leeds-Liverpool Canal just to the east of Burscough, running as far as Tarleton to connect with the River Douglas and the Ribble estuary.

Below: A cornfield near Westhead.

Starting Point: Southport station. Regular trains from Liverpool Central and Moorfields, Wigan Wallgate, Bolton, Manchester Piccadilly, and Manchester Victoria (not Sundays). Motorists should park in Southport (a choice of car parks) and catch the train back from Burscough Bridge.

Finishing/Return Point: Burscough Bridge. Regular trains to Southport, Wigan Wallgate and Manchester Victoria; less frequent to Bolton and Manchester Piccadilly (except Sundays, when all trains run to Bolton and Manchester Piccadilly).

Alternative Finishing Point: Burscough Junction: Trains every 90min (not Sundays) to Ormskirk (connection to Liverpool) and Preston. Hoscar station is also near the end of the route (same trains as for Burscough Bridge, but fewer stop at Hoscar).

Cut-off Point: If you wish to shorten the route you can return from Town Green station, Aughton. Regular trains to Liverpool Moorfields, Liverpool Central and Ormskirk; connection from Ormskirk to Preston (trains every 90min — no Sunday service).

Distance: 38km (23³/₄ miles).

Time: 3¹/₂ hr.

Map: Landranger 108: Liverpool

Surfaces and Gradients: Almost completely tarmac; one section of a few yards is gravel path. Very easy gradients in this part of Lancashire, but one climb of around 40m.

Traffic Conditions: Busy out of Southport, otherwise moderate along generally quiet roads.

Facilities: Cafés: Southport. Pubs: Southport, Town Green, Ring O' Bells, Burscough Bridge. Shops: Southport, Town

Green, Burscough Bridge.
WCs: Southport, Burscough Bridge.
Tourist Information: Southport.

ROUTE INSTRUCTIONS:
From Southport station, exit by the car park on the right. Turn right (away from the town centre) and go down Scarisbrick Street. Follow this road to the next junction then turn left and go straight ahead at the next two junctions until you emerge at the Promenade. Turn left and follow this road as far as the roundabout. Turn right and at the next roundabout turn left (signed for car parks only). (If you want to follow the sea front, go straight ahead instead and follow the concrete promenade which runs parallel to the coastal road.)

The road runs past the Jubilee Nature Reserve before joining the coast road at the next roundabout. Take the second turning and veer off to join the start of the Trans-Pennine Trail (TPT). This cycle lane runs parallel to the coast road. After about 4km (2¹/₂ miles) the TPT bends left and after crossing the Ainsdale road becomes a narrow path for a short distance. It soon regains its surface and its position alongside the coastal road. After crossing the railway, the TPT crosses over the main A565 to Moor Lane; take the bike path which joins the coast road at the junction and go straight ahead at the traffic lights.

Follow Moor Lane as it narrows and becomes Plex Moss Lane. Ignore turn-offs and follow this narrow lane through the open fields. Cross over the A5147 and continue

ROUTE 2
ACROSS THE WEST LANCASHIRE PLAIN
SOUTHPORT TO BURSCOUGH

N

straight ahead on Plex Moss Lane as it crosses the Leeds-Liverpool Canal before twisting southwards to emerge at Rosemary Lane. Turn left and at the next junction turn right, where the road soon meets the B5195.

Turn left and follow this road as it gradually ascends, and at the first roundabout turn right. Cross over the A59 at the roundabout to go straight down Winifred Lane. Turn left at the junction to pass Town Green railway station. At the end of the road turn left and take the next right shortly after.

Follow this lane round as it bends eastwards to meet the A570. Take Scarth Mill Lane opposite. From now on it is easiest to follow the blue cycle signs of the Lancashire Cycleway as far as Westhead; the route turns right then next left, next right and left on to School Lane.

At Westhead turn left away from the Lancashire Cycleway on to the main road.

With great care (restricted view; if in doubt cross by foot) turn right on the bend on to Castle Lane. Follow this lane by the woods and go straight ahead at the next junction. Where the lane ends turn right on to Blythe Lane and follow this road until it meets the B5240 then turn left on to the A5209. (If you are travelling back to Ormskirk, Preston or Merseyside, from Blythe Lane take the first left, Flax Lane, and turn left on to the A5209, then take the next right to Burscough Junction station.)

Take the next right to cross the canal again by the Ring O' Bells pub. Turn left and follow this road into Burscough Bridge. Burscough Bridge station is on the right where you emerge on to the A59.

Below: Southport town centre.

OVER WYRE: POULTON-LE-FYLDE CIRCULAR

This little known coastal part of Lancashire with its narrow lanes, deserted salt marshes and old farmhouses seems a world away from the crowded beaches and ribbon development of Blackpool and Fleetwood just a few miles to the south. Look out for the spectacular views across the Wyre and Lune estuaries to the hills of Bowland.

BACKGROUND AND PLACES OF INTEREST:

Over Wyre

Over Wyre is the name given to the low-lying area of land north of the River Wyre, where salt marshes (with industrial brine wells in many places) give way to rich farmland. Though, inevitably, many of the larger villages have developed as dormitory suburbs of Blackpool, Cleveleys and Fleetwood, much of the character of the area remains, with some charming villages and hamlets.

Poulton-le-Fylde

This ancient town was once a busy little harbour on the Wyre estuary known as 'Pool Town'. The harbour has long silted up but the town has a picturesque market square with a stone cross, and a stocks and whipping post where criminals received rough justice. It is now a busy shopping centre with pedestrian precincts and an indoor market.

Wardley Creek

A delightful backwater on the River Wyre which takes it name from a popular inn. This is now a busy marina, colourful with boats, sails and masts in the creek or passing on the river. Wardley Lane, which links the creek with the hamlet of Staynall, winds between high hedges with fine views across to Fleetwood beyond Staynall.

The Pilling Pig

The railway branch line from Garstang to Pilling was built in 1864 to serve the hitherto isolated community at Pilling, the line being finally completed to Knott End in 1908. One of the little steam locomotives with its mournful whistle became known by local farmers as the 'Pilling Pig', a name which was retained by the whole line until its closure in 1930. The trackbed of the line is still visible and is passed several times on this ride.

Right: Pilling Church.

Knott End-on-Sea

The railway helped transform this little fishing village, just across the river from the bustling port of Fleetwood, into a small seaside resort, with a popular café to attract travellers on the little ferry which still operates in the summer months. It is now a bustling commuter village, still with its strip of promenade, stretch of beach and fine sea views, often with a large container ship bound for Ireland pulling out of Fleetwood harbour adding interest.

Pilling

This lovely old village which was once a centre of the salt-mining industry (the brine wells will be passed on this ride near Preesall) has a fine church and the remains of an old windmill built in 1808 at Damside on the little Broadfleet river. A farm labourer once accepted a wager to be tied to its sails for a barrel of beer, but after one revolution begged to be released. From 1900 the mill was worked by steam.

Lane Ends — the Wyre-Lune Wildfowl Sanctuary

This small but extremely attractive nature reserve is a National Wildfowl Sanctuary. It is managed by the Environment Agency and has a sheltered pond (where ducks and waders are usually to be seen), a picnic area and seats on the embankment offering superb views across Pilling Marsh and Cockerham Sands in the Lune estuary, towards Heysham power station, the Lakeland hills in the distance and, to the east, the rolling summits of the Bowland Fells. It is the perfect place for a short pause to admire this surprisingly lovely stretch of coastline.

Starting Point: Poulton-le-Fylde station, which is very well served by fast trains from Preston, Bolton, Manchester, Blackburn, Accrington, Burnley and West Yorkshire. There is ample car parking in the town. Alternatively, in the summer months (May to October), it is possible to start and end the ride at Fleetwood, taking the hourly ferry across the Wyre to Knott End — cycles carried for just 50p. For exact times ring Lancashire County Council travel line on 0870 608 2608.

Finishing/Return Point: Poulton-le-Fylde.

Distance: 47km (29 miles).

Time: $4^1/_2$ hours.

Map: OS Landranger 102: Preston & Blackpool.

Surfaces and Gradients: All roads or lanes, though some short sections of the lanes have poor or cracked surfaces, where a little care is required. Gradients are all slight, and generally not difficult. Wind may be more of a problem in this exposed coastal area, especially a strong prevailing westerly.

Traffic Conditions: The first and last 3km (2 miles) in and out of Poulton suffer some extremely heavy traffic, especially along the A585/A586 to and across Shard Bridge, which is the only crossing of the lower Wyre. Care is required here. It is busy also around Knott End. Once away from these areas the roads, however, are generally very quiet, with some delightful stretches.

Facilities:
Cafés: Poulton, Knott End, Pilling.
Pubs: Poulton, Hambleton, Wardleys Creek, Preesall, Knott End, Pilling, Stake Pool.
Shops: Poulton, Knott End, Pilling.
WCs: Poulton, Knott End, Pilling.

ROUTE INSTRUCTIONS:
Exit from Poulton station, turn sharp right into Breck Road (this is a one-way street so if you want to go into the centre of Poulton it is best to walk) and go down to the traffic lights. Keep straight ahead, following signs to Over Wyre and Knott End. At the busy traffic island at Skippool on the A585 (M6 link road), follow the red marked cycleway around the island to head eastwards. At the traffic lights after 1km take the cycle filter behind the lights on to the A585 towards Over Wyre and Knott End. The traffic

here is almost as horrendously busy as the previous section, but at least there is a white marked cycleway leading over Shard Bridge into Over Wyre. At the next island turn left towards the village of Hambleton and follow a series of bends right and left into the village centre. At the Shovels Inn, just past a petrol station, turn sharp left along Kiln Lane. This suburban road soon improves as the houses end, with the traffic now vanishing as you head for Wardleys Creek.

This is a delightful spot: an informal marina crowded with colourful boats amid tall rushes. Continue past the Wardley Inn, following Wardley Lane as it swings right and becomes an extremely narrow lane between tall hedges which is sandy in places — an astonishing contrast to the recently left A588. Then follow the lane up and over a gentle hill to the hamlet of Staynall. Turn left here for the Heads and Stalmine, with fine views over the flood banks by Borrows Marsh nature reserve, and across the estuary to Fleetwood. At the next junction turn right along Highgate Lane towards Stalmine, pass the Preesall brine wells in the fields at either side, then left at the next junction, this time heading for Preesall and Knott End. Preesall village is now straight ahead, with a sudden steep climb to join the B5377 in the village centre. Turn left here and head for Knott End-on-Sea, soon joining the B5270 along Bourne May Road.

Knott End is a good place to pause for refreshment and to admire the view. Riders using the ferry from Fleetwood can join the route here, returning as described from Hambleton. Retrace the route through the village for just over 1km looking out for the church on the left, where you turn sharp left (signed to Medical Centre) along Pilling Lane. As the ribbon development finally peters out, this becomes a pleasant rural lane, passing open farmland, with the sea and coast just a field's width away. The lane turns sharp right inland then meanders by farms and stables around a series of zigzags before finally reaching the main A588, here known as Head Dyke Lane. Taking care with the fast traffic, turn left on to the A588 for just under 1km, then turn sharp left along Lambs Lane, signed to the village and Pilling. The lane eventually turns right towards the village centre. Follow the same road into the village centre past a café, church and inn towards Damside and the old mill, but where the road bears right over the bridge keep ahead on a narrow lane parallel with the embankment. Near

Opposite: Wardleys Creek.

the end of this lovely quiet road is the entrance on the left to Lane Ends nature reserve and picnic area.

Continue from the reserve along the lane to the main road. Turn right here but after some 300m, where the road bends right, turn sharp left along Horse Park Lane past Pilling Hall. This pleasant lane takes you past open farmland and eventually emerges in Garstang Road — turn right here to rejoin the main road at Stake Pool. Turn left again at the main road, but where the road bends right, keep ahead on the fork to Bradshaw Lane. At the first junction, near Scronkey, follow the wider road (Lancaster Road) on the right, at the sign for Great Eccleston. At the next junction, Union Lane, turn right towards Hambleton to follow a long, straight road across Pilling Marsh which is suffering from subsidence, so take care. Turn left at the next junction at Hale Nook but where the road sweeps left, bear right (take care at bend) along Clay Gap Lane to Crumbleholme. Turn left here towards Hambleton, but at the next junction take the Out Rawcliffe road straight ahead, then at the next crossing keep towards Hambleton again. (If you are returning to Knott End this way follow this route into Hambleton centre then follow the route as described above from the Shovels Inn.) At the next junction at Grove Lane turn left, this time for Poulton and Blackpool, later going right at the T-junction along Ghants Lane towards Shard Bridge.

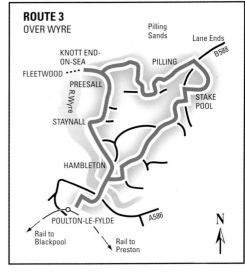

ROUTE 3
OVER WYRE

This emerges at the traffic island below Hambleton. Head along the cycle lane over Shard Bridge to the traffic lights and take the awkward turn right along the A585 to Skippool Island, keeping left along the cycle track filter towards Poulton. At the traffic lights below Poulton go up Station Road, taking the first right past the railway bridge to the town centre, with the railway station (signed) along Breck Road to the right.

🚲 ROUTE 4

FYLDE TO THE RIBBLE: KIRKHAM AND WESHAM TO LANGHO

In its first stages this ride crosses the flat, richly arable countryside of the Fylde peninsula, with its market gardens and glasshouses. Heading eastwards and ascending to Inglewhite, the route cuts across the edge of the Bowland foothills to emerge in lower Ribblesdale. A short ride takes you to the fascinating Roman military town of Ribchester, then across the Ribble to Langho, on the Ribble Valley line.

BACKGROUND AND PLACES OF INTEREST:

Kirkham
Kirkham is an ancient town inhabited at least since Roman times, as evidenced by the remains of a Roman settlement on Mill Hill. In 1296 the Abbey of Vale Royal granted Kirkham a charter making its inhabitants free men who could hold fairs and a market. The town was actually built in the form of a cross, with the market place in the centre. Ancient fish stones, from where fish were sold, stand in the market square and there is still a weekly market every Thursday.

Bilsborrow
A picturesque village on the Lancaster Canal, noted for its old inns and canalside walks.

Longridge
The town of Longridge, with its shops and facilities, is dominated by the huge bulk of Longridge Fell, an outlier of the Bowland Fells. Longridge Fell rises to the immediate east of the town and from it there are magnificent views of

The Roman Bath House, Ribchester.

the whole of the Fylde plain and the surrounding Bowland Fells. It was once famous as a quarrying centre, with stone from local sandstone quarries being carried to build the town hall of Lancaster and Liverpool docks.

Ribchester
As its name implies, Ribchester, on the banks of the Ribble, was an ancient Roman town, known as Bremetennacum. The excellent Roman Museum contains displays about Roman life, illustrated by many important finds made in the village, including a Roman helmet found in 1796. It is an attractive town, with Georgian and Victorian houses, inns and shops, and a pleasant area of riverbank.

Langho
There are two parts of the village, more than two kilometres apart. Old Langho has a church which dates from the 1550s, and was build from stone plundered from nearby Whalley Abbey, including a carved stone table. New Langho, now simply called Langho, is a more modern village and commuter settlement; it has a recently reopened railway station on the Ribble Valley line.

Starting Point: Kirkham & Wesham station. Trains run hourly between Preston, Kirkham and Blackpool South. Motorists should park in Preston, take the outward train to Kirkham and return from Langho to Preston.

ROUTE 4
FYLDE TO THE RIBBLE
KIRKHAM & WESHAM TO RIBCHESTER AND LANGHO

Rail to Lancaster

BILSBORROW

To Inglewhite

A6

M6

B5269

CATFORTH

M55

Lancaster Canal

Rail to Blackpool North

TREALES

Rail to Blackpool South

A585

Stn
KIRKHAM & WESHAM

PRESTON Stn

Rail to Blackburn, Manchester

N

Finishing/Return Point: Langho. There is an hourly train service to Blackburn on the Ribble Valley (Blackburn-Clitheroe) line, with frequent connections to Preston.

Distance: 40km (25 miles).

Time: 4 hours.

Maps: OS Landranger 102: Preston & Blackpool; 103: Blackburn & Burnley.

Surfaces and Gradients: Good tarmac surfaces throughout. The first part has easy gradients, but there are some hillier sections as you approach the Ribble Valley.

Traffic Conditions: Mainly quiet lanes with fairly light traffic, but there are some busy sections where care is required, especially crossing the main roads.

Facilities:
Cafés: Kirkham, Wesham, Inglewhite (Wed-Sun).
Pubs: Kirkham, Wesham, Treales, Kidsnape, Inglewhite, Bilsborrow, Longridge, Ribchester, Old Langho.
Shops: Kirkham, Ribchester, Longridge.
WCs: Longridge, Ribchester.

ROUTE INSTRUCTIONS:
From Kirkham station turn right to go into its twin village of Wesham (if you wish to explore Kirkham, turn left from the station), and take the second right which is Derby Road. Follow this past the hospital grounds and turn left up Park Lane just before the end of the road. Follow Park Lane until the end then turn right on to Mowbreck Lane.

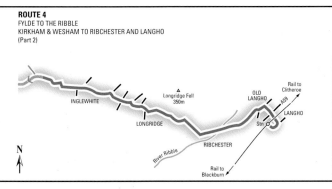

ROUTE 4
FYLDE TO THE RIBBLE
KIRKHAM & WESHAM TO RIBCHESTER AND LANGHO
(Part 2)

This narrow road becomes a track by a farm then emerges at a cross-roads. Go straight ahead, passing the hamlet of Treales and, further on, the Hand and Dagger pub by the Lancaster Canal.

Take the third turn left after the pub, Blackleach Lane. At the next junction, turn right, still on Blackleach Lane which crosses over the canal by means of a hump-backed bridge, then turn left when you meet the main road. Take the next right at Catforth, continuing as far as the B5269. Take the next right, Eaves Lane, by the farm at Black Pole.

Follow the lane as it is joined by Cinder Lane before crossing New Mill Bridge; after the bridge take the second left. This lane bends sharp right by a dead-end sign; continue along Malley Lane until the end. Turn left as the lane winds roughly northeastwards. At the next junction turn right to head into Bilsborrow.

Turn left on to the A6 and take the next right (between the two pubs). The road rises gradually and crosses the main railway line and the M6 motorway, before climbing again. Ignore the turn-offs and continue to Inglewhite.

From Inglewhite continue straight ahead to Longridge. At the junction turn right then left up the slope into Longridge town centre. At the top turn left and follow the main B road out towards Ribchester. The Clitheroe road turns off, so continue on the B6245 to Ribchester as it makes its long gradual descent into the Ribble Valley. In Ribchester the Roman Museum can be reached by continuing straight ahead (it is clearly signed) where the main road turns sharp left.

Leave Ribchester on the B6245 and follow this as far as the bridge over the River Ribble, 1km (½ mile) further on. Take the narrow lane immediately on the left over the bridge. This lane runs along the floodplain before a short but stiff climb past Salesbury Hall and into the surrounding woods. Follow this lane until it meets another lane. Turn left and continue as far as Old Langho, turning right at the pub. (If you wish to go to Whalley instead, follow this lane round until it ends at a T-junction and turn left to go down to Whalley.)

The lane climbs gently towards Langho — cross the busy A59 using the traffic island provided for cyclists. Continue into Langho and turn right by the railway bridge. Follow the main road a short distance (caution needed), looking out for the station sign down the lane which you should follow to the railway station.

RIVINGTON PIKE AND BELMONT: BLACKROD TO ENTWISTLE (OR BROMLEY CROSS)

Rivington is a popular cyclists' destination on the slopes of the great moorland ridge that forms Winter Hill, one of the outliers of the West Pennine Moors. Although this route is only 18km (11¼ miles) long, it allows for the fact that most cyclists will want to explore Lever Park, perhaps on foot as well as by cycle. The moorland road over the back of Winter Hill to Belmont gives some breathtaking views. Entwistle station, where this ride ends, also has the celebrated real-ale Strawbury Duck Inn. Alternatively, the ride can easily be extended through Turton Bottoms and Jumbles Country Park to Bromley Cross.

BACKGROUND AND PLACES OF INTEREST:

Lever Park

Lord Leverhulme, the Lancashire soap magnate, gave this magnificent hillside estate with its castle and great park to the people of Bolton in 1902. It is an ever popular countryside destination, containing a replica of Liverpool's medieval castle, the Georgian Rivington Hall, two magnificent cruck-barns and areas of grassland, tracks and paths overlooking the Rivington reservoirs, as well as the celebrated and recently restored Terraced Gardens. The Great House Barn has information, refreshments and toilets, Rivington Hall Barn also has a licensed restaurant and there are several walking trails, as well as bridlepaths where cycling is permitted,

Rivington Pike

Rivington Pike tower, 330m (1,191ft) above sea level, is a landmark for many miles across Lancashire, and can be seen from many places on this ride. Built in 1733, it marks the site of one of the ancient chain of beacons used to transmit dramatic national news of events such as the coming of the Spanish Armada in 1588. The nearby summit of Winter Hill, with its television transmitter, continues the hill's traditional role of keeping the people of the region informed of current events.

Belmont Village

This attractive West Pennine moorland village lies around an old bleaching and dyeing works. An obelisk in Maria Square in the village commemorates the struggle of local workers in the 1820s to get a village water supply from the local Wards Reservoir which supplied the works but not local people.

Jumbles Country Park

This is an area of attractive countryside around the Bradshaw Valley and the Turton & Entwistle and Wayoh reservoirs, with a choice of old pack-horse ways and walking trails. There is a local history museum in 15th century Turton Tower (on the B6391 beyond Turton Bottoms).

Above: Sunset over Wayoh Reservoir, near Entwistle.

Above right: The replica of Liverpool Castle in Lever Park.

Right: The Strawbury Duck Inn, Entwistle.

Starting Point: Blackrod. Hourly trains from Bolton and Manchester Piccadilly. Motorists are advised to park in Bolton, taking an outward train to Blackrod and returning from Entwistle or Bromley Cross.

Finishing/Return Point: Entwistle station. Several trains a day call between Manchester Victoria and Blackburn; the services are more frequent in the afternoon and evening. If no convenient train is available, Bromley Cross is only 3km (c2 miles) away (6km [3¾ miles] via Edgworth and Turton Bottoms), from where there are hourly trains to Bolton, Manchester Victoria and Blackburn.

Distance: 18km (11¼ miles). Bromley Cross is 21km (13 miles).

Time: 2½ hours (plus time to explore Lever Park).

Map: OS Landranger 109: Manchester & Surrounding Area.

Surfaces and Gradients: The route is nearly all on tarmac roads with two very short sections of rough track. It is generally undulating with one steep ascent of 200 metres across the Rivington ridge, and a number of other shorter, steep climbs.

Traffic Conditions: Traffic is fairly busy (care required) from Blackrod to Horwich, light in Lever Park and to Belmont, and moderate to Entwistle.

Facilities:
Cafés: Rivington Barn Visitor Centre, Rivington.
Pubs: Blackrod, Horwich, Belmont, Entwistle.
Shops: Blackrod, Horwich.
WCs: Rivington Barn and Hall, Belmont.

ROUTE DESCRIPTION:

Turn left from Blackrod station exit taking the B5238 into Horwich as far as the roundabout. Turn left at the roundabout and take the next right into Lever Park Avenue, which is distinguished by a stone obelisk.

Follow this road as it leaves town, soon passing through woodland above Rivington Reservoir. After about 2km (1¼ miles) turn right on the road signed for Rivington Hall and climb up past the car park bays to the hall. Continue up to the highest car park, past the picnic tables. You may wish to park your cycle in this area to explore the park's facilities on foot.

From the car park go straight ahead through low wooden posts on to a path which leads through an avenue of trees to a track. The track runs along a fence to a gate and a road. Turn right as the road climbs gently, and take the turn for Belmont at the next junction. The road climbs more steeply on to and across Rivington Moor and crosses a saddle in the moors before a spectacular and fast descent down to Belmont village.

At the junction turn right, then take the next left down a steep narrow lane which quickly regains height to emerge at a crossroads. Go straight ahead and follow the road, ignoring a turn-off to the right as you pass through plantations of pine trees, and gain height to meet the busy A666. Turn left with great care on to this main road and turn right about 500m further on to the B6391.

Follow the B6391 as it emerges from the spruce plantations and begins to descend the hillside. Take the second turn-off left and follow this lane down to Entwistle Reservoir.

(For the most direct route to Bromley Cross, continue along the B6391 into the village; the station is on the right near the base of the hill. Alternatively, follow the lane via Wayoh Reservoir to Edgworth, turning right via Turton Bottoms and Jumbles Country Park to rejoin the B6391 for Bromley Cross.)

Continue across the reservoir on the road to where it becomes a rough track on the other bank, and enters the hamlet of Entwistle. The track emerges by the Strawbury Duck Inn next to the station entrance.

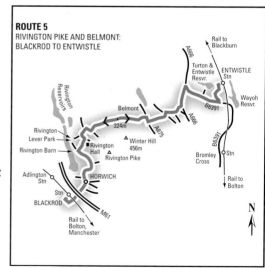

ROUTE 5
RIVINGTON PIKE AND BELMONT:
BLACKROD TO ENTWISTLE

🚲 ROUTE 6

SECRET WAYS IN CENTRAL LANCASHIRE: BLACKBURN TO CHORLEY

Central Lancashire is not all urban development and motorways. In between the concrete and brick are some delightful stretches of countryside and quiet lanes. This ride from Blackburn to Chorley along the valley of the River Darwen takes in some astonishingly unspoiled countryside, quiet back lanes and tracks, and has some spectacular views.

BACKGROUND AND PLACES OF INTEREST:

Blackburn

Blackburn is a large industrial town with some impressive public buildings, including the cathedral with its striking modern corona. Its rich industrial heritage links both the engineering and the cotton industries. If you have time it is worth exploring Eanam Wharf on the Leeds-Liverpool Canal, with its craft workshops, the fine Blackburn Museum, and the Lewis Textile Museum. The town is also an important hub on the local rail network, making access easy from a wide area of Lancashire.

Witton Country Park

This 194-hectare country park has extensive woodland, open rough grassland and playing field areas, all with a choice of walks and trails. There is a visitor centre (open mainly afternoons; Sundays from 11am) with local and natural history displays. There are tea rooms at the Stables Visitor Centre and at the Pavilion (where there are also toilets). Cyclists are requested to keep to the main tarmac track, cycle slowly and give way to pedestrians in the park.

The visitor centre at Witton Country Park.

Pleasington Old Hall Woods Nature Reserve

Attractive mixed woodland along the side of a stream forms the main feature of this small reserve, with an old walled garden which is notable for butterflies and other wildlife. The area is also noted for a variety of birds including nuthatches and woodpeckers. Access is on foot only, so cycles should be left outside the reserve area.

Pleasington

A quiet, former weavers' village on the outskirts of Blackburn which also has a local rail station on the Blackburn-Preston line, enabling this ride to be shortened by some 7km (4 miles). It is also home to Pleasington Priory, a Roman Catholic church built in a grand Gothic style at the time of Catholic emancipation in 1819.

Samlesbury Hall

The richly half-timbered Samlesbury Hall, though heavily restored, is a superb example of 14th century domestic architecture, set in $2^1/_2$ hectares of landscaped grounds. Built in 1325, the hall has a fine oriel window, a banqueting hall and a minstrels' gallery. It is now a popular craft and antiques exhibition centre. The hall is open daily except Mondays; there is an admission charge.

Chorley

A busy town which has had a market charter since 1498, a tradition which continues with its famous Tuesday 'Flat Iron' market. Despite much modern development, cycle-unfriendly ring roads and car parks, the character of the old town survives along its partly pedestrianised main street with shops, cafés and pubs, and a parish church which dates from 1360.

Starting Point: Blackburn railway station. There are frequent trains from Manchester, Bolton, Blackpool, Preston, Burnley and Clitheroe. Anyone coming by car is advised to park either in Bolton or Preston and catch the train to Blackburn to simplify the return journey by train.

Finishing/Return Point: Chorley station. There are trains every few minutes on weekdays (less frequently on Sundays so check times) to Bolton, Manchester, Preston (change at Preston for Blackburn) and Blackpool.

Distance: 32km (20 miles).

Time: $3^1/_2$ hours.

Maps: OS Landranger 109: Manchester; 102: Preston & Blackpool; 103: Blackburn & Burnley.

Surfaces and Gradients: A wide range from main roads to steep, unsurfaced tracks where walking is advised, but mostly the route is on quiet lanes with good surfaces. There are several steep sections where the route crosses the Darwen Valley and its tributaries, making this a moderately strenuous ride.

Above: Samlesbury Hall.

Traffic Conditions: There are busy urban roads at the beginning and end of the ride and two very short stretches of the A677 and A675 where care is required crossing the road. Otherwise, all is on quiet lanes or tracks.

Facilities:
Cafés: Blackburn, Witton Country Park, Samlesbury Hall (restaurant), Chorley.
Pubs: Blackburn, Pleasington, Samlesbury Bottom (Nab's Head), Hoghton, Wheelton (Top Lock), Chorley.
Shops: Blackburn, Chorley.
WCs: Blackburn, Witton Country Park, Chorley.
Tourist Information: Blackburn.

ROUTE INSTRUCTIONS:

From Blackburn station entrance turn left along Jubilee Street following the one-way system past the bus station to the traffic lights. Turn left here along Darwen Street. After 120m, where there is a triangular traffic island on the right (keep to the right-hand lane if you can), turn right along Weir Street. At the end of this road turn right past the solitary Gothic church tower until you reach more traffic lights. Turn left here into King Street. Continue past the next set of lights, and 100m beyond them turn right up Stonyhurst Road into a 20mph zone. At the junction by the Three Pigeons Inn turn left along Wensley Road, now part of the Witton Park Cycleway as indicated by blue signs, with cycle priority gates. Continue past the Lion Inn to the junction with St Mark's Road. Go left here, then take the first right (again following the blue Witton Park cycle signs) into Rollston Road, then go left at the next junction, by the shops, towards St Mark's Church with its unusual tower. Turn left on the main road, but almost immediately look for the signs for Witton Park, down a fairly modest entrance drive a few metres on the right. Follow the long entrance drive (giving way to pedestrians) down into the park, heading beyond the car park and gateposts along the track to the visitor centre on the right.

From the visitor centre follow the main drive left which leads past the playing fields and Pavilion (with café) to the southern entrance of the park and on to the busy A674. Cross and turn right here, climbing steeply uphill some 300m to where the road bends left. A minor road, signed to Pleasington Nature Reserve (Tower Road), leads straight ahead. Take care here, this is a dangerous turn across the line of traffic. The lane drops steeply down into the entrance to Pleasington Park, past playing fields.

The lane now climbs towards the cemetery on the hillside above, soon reaching the nature reserve (the entrance is by the footpath on the left). Continue to just before a small pond on the left where the track goes below the pond (no right to cycle here but there is a parallel footpath that a cycle can be wheeled along that joins the track). This track joins Old Hall Lane, a narrow tarmac lane. Follow this lane to where it joins Sandy Lane on the edge of Pleasington. Turn left for Pleasington Priory and the Butlers Arms Inn.

Return to the junction with Old Hall Lane. The route continues northwards, on a very steep descent before an equally steep climb up Woodcock Hill. Ignore the junction part way up, but cross the brow of the hill where the road swings sharply right, with a partly whitewashed cottage (Temple Close) on the corner. To the left is an unmarked lane which looks like a private road. Where it forks, keep right and bear right again by a house entrance where an overgrown, almost tree-covered, bridlepath drops steeply into the woods. This ancient stony lane is a steep, slippery (walking is strongly advised for this 500m stretch) but extremely beautiful way through dense woodland. Descend to a bridge,

ROUTE 6
SECRET WAYS IN CENTRAL LANCASHIRE

then climb the steep bridlepath, now very narrow in places (a challenge to even the most determined mountain biker), before finally joining a small, traffic-free lane with the evocative name of Further Lane. This is easy, delightful cycling to the hamlet of Nab's Head, a community which takes it name from the pub. Turn right along Nab's Head Lane, keeping ahead at the next junction to eventually reach the busy A677. Cross this fast main road carefully, and turn right. The entrance to Samlesbury Hall is 80m on the left.

Return along the same route to Nab's Head (if omitting the visit to Samlesbury Hall, 3km or 2 miles is saved), this time taking the lane on the right, Goosefoot Lane, which drops steeply down to Samlesbury Bottoms — an old water mill and a collection of cottages. A very steep ascent from the bottoms eventually leads to a T-junction. Turn right here following the signs to Hoghton, and right again at the next junction along Gib's Lane (superb views across the Pennine foothills to the Lancashire Plain and Preston from here), going under the railway line to join the A675 Old Blackburn Road at the Boar's Head Inn.

Cross the road and turn right for just 100m until you reach a junction at the edge of Hoghton village. Turn left here towards Brindle, and sharp left again after another 30 metres along Gouns Lane. Go left at the next T-junction, keeping right at the next fork along Windmill Lane, another very steep climb, turning right at the top of the hill to descend past Windmill Hill Farm and join the B5256. Turn left here for 250m then, as the road bends left, look for a narrow lane on the right. This soon crosses the M65 and climbs steadily uphill, with ever more impressive views of the West Pennine Moors and Rivington Pike, eventually reaching a hamlet consisting of a single row of terraced houses known as Top o'th'Hill. Now follows an exhilarating descent to almost meet the M61; turn left at the T-junction down to a bridge in a wooded valley, the road now climbing steeply uphill to the Leeds-Liverpool Canal and the Top Lock inn below Wheelton. Follow the road round as it swings south towards Chorley. At the next junction, turn right then first left along the unmarked Dark Lane.

Just before Dark Lane joins a feeder link road for new industrial development, look for blue cycleway signs left to Chorley which direct cyclists along a stretch of old road leading to a huge new traffic island in the dual carriageway complex. Follow the cycleway and pedestrian way around the huge island, heading for the B674, the old Blackburn Road into Chorley.

Chorley isn't the nicest town to cycle into, with its ribbon development. Go along the undulating old main road which crosses the M61 and Leeds-Liverpool Canal, leading up to a busy traffic island on the edge of the town. Do not follow the town centre signs which lead

to an unpleasant dual carriageway system, but turn left along the urban road signed for Anglezarke and Adlington. Keep ahead for around 1km, pass the Derby Hotel and two pelican crossings until you reach a minor road, Brown Street (marked as a cul-de-sac) on the right, opposite a new housing estate and old iron railings. A line of posts stops cars but cyclists can continue along this suburban road which leads straight ahead down to the railway line where another cycle-unfriendly one-way tunnel (walk the 50m to save a very long detour) leads to the clutter of car parks that passes for the entrance to Chorley station on your left.

Above right: Pleasington Priory.

Right: A distant view of Preston from a lane near Hoghton.

🚲 ROUTE 7

THE TROUGH OF BOWLAND: CLITHEROE TO LANCASTER

This is a classic ride through the heart of the Forest of Bowland. The ride starts in Clitheroe and turns away from Pendle, heading northwards over the River Ribble before taking a gentle but steady climb through Bashall Eaves towards Browsholme Hall. The route then drops down into the beautiful wooded Hodder Valley and follows this as far as Dunsop Bridge — a hamlet nestling within the Bowland Fells. The next section is through the moors and an undulating approach leads to a steep ascent over the Trough of Bowland watershed. Once over the pass, a fast gradual descent follows into the upper Wyre Valley. The ride follows the north side of this valley with views of the coast as the moors are left behind. A further descent into Galgate crosses the main M6 and West Coast main line railway before the final section along the rolling lowland northwards to Lancaster.

Below: The Trough of Bowland.
North West Tourist Board

BACKGROUND AND PLACES OF INTEREST:

Forest of Bowland Area of Outstanding Natural Beauty

One of the largest and most spectacular AONBs in the north of England, the Forest of Bowland actually has very little forest — the name refers to an ancient hunting reserve. It is open fell country, mostly with heather moor and rough grazing, interspersed with water catchment reservoirs and penetrated by a number of extremely beautiful, narrow river valleys (including the Hodder Valley which is followed on this ride) where there are a number of unspoiled villages. The Ribble Valley divides the main Bowland area from its dramatic eastern outlier, Pendle Hill (see Routes 8 and 10).

Clitheroe
For details see Route 8.

Browsholme Hall

This fine Tudor mansion is the historic family seat of the Parkers, Bow-Bearers of the Forest of Bowland. One member of the family, Thomas Parker, became Lord Chancellor of England and his portrait hangs in the picture collection, alongside wood carvings, period furniture, textiles, rare books, arms and armour. The house is open to the public at certain times in the summer months.

Whitewell
This attractive village, with its church, inn and scattered cottages, stands on a narrow, wooded curve of the River Hodder. The area is known locally as Little Switzerland.

Dunsop Bridge
It is claimed by the Ordnance Survey that the pretty village of Dunsop Bridge is the nearest village to the exact centre of the British Isles and a commemorative public telephone box on the village green has been erected to mark this fact. A painting of a racehorse on the ceiling above the altar of St Hubert's Church is said to be of the Derby winner Kettledrum, owned by the Townley family, whose winnings on the horse paid for the building of the church.

Trough of Bowland
This spectacular, steep and narrow pass linking the Hodder, Wyre and Lune valleys is a favourite stopping point of cyclists before an exhilarating descent into the Lune Valley. The pass squeezes its way between Blaze Moss and Whins Brow, offering spectacular views westwards across to Blackpool and the coast, and northwestwards to Lancaster.

Abbeystead
The picturesque village of Abbeystead takes its name from a Cistercian abbey which was established, probably close to where the two Wyre rivers join, by the monks of Furness Abbey in the 12th century although the monks moved on to Ireland shortly afterwards. Nearby Abbeystead House is the shooting home of the Duke of Westminster, who owns the extensive Abbeystead grouse moors.

Dolphinholme
Dolphinholme is a fascinating early Industrial Revolution mill village. Its worsted mill was established in 1787, originally to take advantage of waterpower on the River Wyre before being converted to steam. The mill once employed over a thousand people, with woolcombing taking place in their houses. In later years it became a cotton mill, and was one of the first mills in England to use coal gas for lighting and heat.

Lancaster
For details see Route 13.

Right: Lancaster Castle.

Starting Point: Clitheroe. Hourly trains on the Ribble Valley line from Blackburn, Preston, Bolton and Manchester Victoria (less frequent on Sundays). Motorists should park in Preston, take the train to Clitheroe and return from Lancaster direct to Preston.

Finishing/Return Point: Lancaster station. There are hourly trains to Bolton, Barrow, Manchester Piccadilly and Wigan as well as frequent services to Preston and Morecambe.

Distance: 50km (31 miles).

Time: 5 hours.

Maps: OS Landranger 103: Blackburn & Burnley; 102: Preston & Blackpool; 97: Kendal & Morecambe.

Surfaces and Gradients: The route takes place all on tarmac roads. There are easy gradients between Clitheroe and Dunsop Bridge; a steep climb (17% or 1:6) to the Trough of Bowland; downhill to Galgate and easy gradients into Lancaster.

Traffic Conditions: On weekdays the roads are fairly quiet with mainly local and some tourist traffic. They can be very busy with tourist traffic on fine Sunday afternoons.

Facilities:
Cafés: Clitheroe, Whitewell, Lancaster.
Pubs: Clitheroe, Whitewell, Dunsop Bridge, Dolphinholme, Galgate, Lancaster.
Shops: Clitheroe, Dunsop Bridge, Galgate, Lancaster.
WCs: Clitheroe, Dunsop Bridge, Lancaster.
Tourist Information: Clitheroe, Lancaster.
Youth Hostel: Slaidburn (7km [4^1/$_3$ miles] east of Dunsop Bridge).

ROUTE INSTRUCTIONS:

Exit from Clitheroe station (northbound platform), turning left away from the town centre into Castle View towards the castle. Bear left at the next junction on to the B6243. Turn right on to the B6243 and follow it over the River Ribble, and take the turning right for Bashall Eaves after ascending the slope.

Continue along this road through Bashall Eaves, following the road signs. The road gains height steadily. Keep on this road signed for Lancaster as it then descends through more open fields. Turn right at the junction and follow this lane as it enters the Hodder Valley and passes through woodland below Whitewell. Continue on this lane as it winds up the valley and crosses the river to pass Dunsop Bridge. Dunsop Bridge is to the right, and is a pleasant place for a break, otherwise continue along the road as it enters the moorland and starts climbing. Some height is lost before the main climb to the Trough of Bowland starts. Follow the road as it gradually ascends over the pass and down into the Wyre Valley, taking the left turn for Abbeystead by the Methodist church about 6km (4 miles) beyond the pass summit.

The road soon descends steeply (caution!) into the hamlet of Abbeystead before ascending again. Continue along this road as far as Dolphinholme. At the double roundabout turn left and then take the second turning, for Galgate. The road bends right and at the crossroads turn right for Galgate and continue straight ahead past the turn-off down into Galgate.

In Galgate go straight ahead at the traffic lights over the A6 to take the road which goes under the railway bridge. Bend right as the lane follows the railway and climbs out of the village. Take the next left down a very narrow lane to join the A588. Turn right on to the A588 and take the second left, a narrow lane concealed between houses. This short lane joins another

lane (also off the A588 if you missed this!) so turn left on to it and follow it to the T-junction. Turn right and follow this lane through the village of Aldcliffe.

The road runs parallel to the canal as it approaches Lancaster. Immediately under the railway bridge turn left into Brook Street which leads into the traffic-calmed Dallas Road. Keep to the left of the traffic humps for comfort, noting the cycleway right into the city centre along High Street. Otherwise turn left along Meeting House Lane to the railway station.

Below: The Lancaster Canal in Lancaster.

ROUTE 7
TROUGH OF BOWLAND: CLITHEROE TO LANCASTER

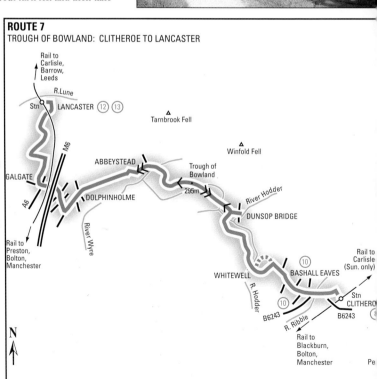

SAWLEY ABBEY AND RIBBLESDALE: CLITHEROE CIRCULAR

This ride through the quiet, undulating countryside of Ribblesdale has equal claim to be in both Lancashire and Yorkshire. It starts from the bustling market town of Clitheroe but soon enters what was part of the old West Riding, by Sawley Abbey and Gisburn, then follows the Ribble into North Yorkshire at Wigglesworth and Hellifield, giving superb views of Yorkshire's Three Peaks and Lancashire's Pendle Hill throughout.

BACKGROUND AND PLACES OF INTEREST:

Clitheroe

Despite the huge cement works and chimneys that dominates the east of the town, Clitheroe has kept its character as a bustling market town with its winding main street with attractive shops, old pubs and friendly cafés. Its spectacular Norman castle (ruined but well worth a visit — open most days) perched on a limestone crag offers a superb viewpoint. There is a helpful tourist information centre on the main street, and its good rail service makes it an excellent base for exploring the Ribble Valley and nearby Pendle country.

Sawley Abbey

Founded in the year 1147 by Baron Percy, grandson of William de Perci who came to England with the Conqueror, Sawley is one of the oldest abbeys in the north. The Cistercian abbey prospered until the Dissolution when its last Abbot, William Trafford, was arrested for his support for the Catholic Pilgrimage of Grace and executed at Lancaster in 1537. The abbey was ruthlessly pillaged for building stone and only fragments of archways and walls remain but, now protected by English Heritage (entrance is free), they have a gaunt beauty. It is a good place to sit and rest.

Hellifield

Once an important Victorian railway junction, and now dominated by traffic on the A65 trunk road, even if you are not catching a train it is worth travelling the extra quarter of a mile to the best surviving Midland Railway station in England. On the celebrated Leeds-Settle-Carlisle line, the station, with its elegant canopies and newly restored refreshment rooms, is open weekends for coffee, snacks and railway memorabilia.

Gisburn

This attractive village was once famous for its cattle market. Gisburn Park, past the route, is the ancestral home of the Lord of Ribblesdale, of the Lister family. The last of the famous Gisburn herd of wild white cattle died in 1857, but a celebrated landscape painting with a white Gisburn bull at Malham Cove painted by James Ward in 1811 hangs in the Tate Gallery.

Downham

For information, see Route 10.

Below: Sawley Abbey.

Starting Point: Clitheroe station, terminus of the Ribble Valley line from Manchester, Bolton and Blackburn, with hourly services weekdays, less frequent Sundays; there is ample car parking nearby. On summer Sundays the Lancashire Dales Rail service provides an afternoon/early return from Hellifield, but cyclists from the Lancaster or Skipton direction can use the Leeds-Morecambe line (four trains per day) and start the ride from Hellifield's magnificent Victorian station.

Finishing/Return Point: Clitheroe or Hellifield.

Distance: 51km (31³/₄ miles).

Time: 4¹/₂ hours.

Map: OS Landranger 103: Blackburn & Burnley.

Surfaces and Gradients: Good surfaces throughout. There are some steady climbs with one or two quite steep ascents and descents across tributary valleys of the Ribble so this is a moderately strenuous ride.

Traffic Conditions: Generally light, but busy with local traffic in and out of Clitheroe, and along the A682 and (especially) the A65 at Hellifield.

Facilities:
Cafés: Ingleton, Gisburn, Hellifield (railway station — weekends only).
Pubs: Clitheroe, Waddington, West Bradford, Grindleton, Sawley, Wigglesworth, Hellifield, Gisburn, Rimington, Downham.
Shops: Clitheroe, Hellifield, Gisburn.
WCs: Clitheroe, Hellifield, Gisburn, Downham.
Tourist Information: Clitheroe.

ROUTE INSTRUCTIONS:
Immediately by the entrance of Clitheroe station turn sharp left through the tunnel under the railway following the signs to the Hellifield platform and the long-stay car park. Go right along a street of terraced houses to join the main Waddington road (B6478) which is busy with local traffic. Turn left, soon descending to cross Brungerly Bridge and then up to the pretty village of Waddington. Just past the church, fork right steeply uphill to a junction at which you should turn right along the lane to West Bradford.

This is a pleasant lane parallel to the Ribble, which soon passes through the village of West Bradford. Keep ahead following the signs to Bolton by Bowland; notice the huge cement works dominating the view across the valley. At the junction with the Chatburn road keep left up a steep hill to Grindleton, then bear right following the signs to Bolton along an undulating road, with superb views across to Pendle Hill, which eventually drops sharply to the bridge at Sawley. Turn right over the bridge bearing right past the Spread Eagle pub — an opening on the left in the wall gives access to Sawley Abbey.

Return to Sawley Bridge, this time following the road to the right as it climbs gently, following the river valley upstream past Bolton Peel. Just before Bolton by Bowland take the lane on the left, signed for Settle. The lane eventually descends to cross the Tosside Beck at Forest Becks, then follows a long and fairly steady climb, rewarded by fine views along Ribblesdale to the Three Peaks as you eventually cross the brow of the hill and join the Slaidburn road near Wigglesworth. Turn right for a sharp and exhilarating descent (take care) through Wigglesworth, sweeping round to the river at Cow Bridge. Immediately over the bridge look for a narrow lane on the right, signed to Hellifield, which goes between water meadows to eventually ascend to the A682. Taking care with fast-moving traffic, follow this road for about a mile. Ignore the first road with a traffic sign (Gallaber Farm only) and as you climb a hill look out for a totally unmarked narrow lane with a soil-covered entrance. This lovely little tarmac way takes you under the Clitheroe–Hellifield railway into the centre of Hellifield. Turn sharp left before the junction behind the Black Bull and by the fish and chip shop which brings you to the A65. It is worth coping with the traffic for 200m, going under the railway, to reach the station drive and visit the grand old station. A winding underpass brings you directly on to the station platforms (with a café ahead).

Above: Clitheroe Castle.

ROUTE 8
SAWLEY ABBEY

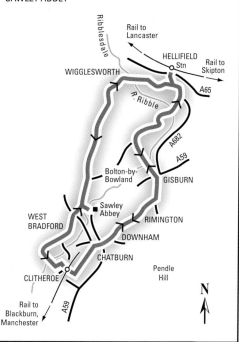

left along the A682 for 400m then take the quiet lane on the right, signed to Halton West.

This is a particularly beautiful road, gently ascending past Halton West village. At the first junction turn left for Bolton by Bowland, following the lane right where it forms the Lancashire-Yorkshire boundary over Paythorne Moor. Keep ahead at the next junction, which is on the summit, and, still following the Bolton signs, the lane bears left and descends past Tewitt House. Take the next lane left, signed to Gisburn. This is Carter's Lane, a narrow route through an archway of trees. At the junction with the main road from Bolton, turn left, descending to the bridge over the Ribble, and then go up a very steep climb to join the A59 in the centre of Gisburn.

Turn left into the village centre, then take the first right along the A682. There is a steady climb for almost a mile until, soon past the brow of the hill, a lane bears right to Rimington. This is a pretty but steeply undulating road on a low ridge up to Rimington. Then go sharply down to Downham Bridge and up to the crossroads with the Chatburn road. It is worth visiting Downham village 400m to the left, but there is a steep climb back along the Chatburn road. Follow the road as it crosses over the A59 into Chatburn. Go directly ahead along the main road, with fairly heavy traffic, into Clitheroe and follow the signs for the station and central car parks.

Return from the station (or start the ride here), go down the underpass and along the drive and turn left on to the A65, going first right after the railway bridge towards Gisburn (there is a short-cut past the fish and chip shop and the loos). Turn

Below: May blossom along the Ribble near Waddington.

BOWLAND KNOTTS AND CROSS OF GREET: BENTHAM CIRCULAR

By any standards this is a strenuous route, not in terms of distance but because of the long and occasionally steep ascents of two high moorland passes across the very heart of the Forest of Bowland Area of Outstanding Natural Beauty. The rewards are some of the most spectacular, panoramic views in Lancashire, across to the peaks of the Yorkshire Dales and into the Ribble Valley and even across to the coast. The delightful village of Slaidburn, popular with cyclists, makes the perfect focal point for a day's ride.

BACKGROUND AND PLACES OF INTEREST:

Bentham

Even though it is administratively in North Yorkshire, and lies on the edge of the Yorkshire Dales, Bentham looks more towards Lancaster down the Wenning and Lune than towards Settle or Skipton in Yorkshire. The village is split into two: High Bentham, the main village with its fine church, railway station and former silk works, and Low Bentham, a smaller village community on the River Wenning about a mile away. High Bentham has an attractive, winding main street with shops, pubs and a café.

Bowland Knotts

This celebrated Bowland pass, which rises to 422m, takes its name from the series of gritstone crags or 'knotts' (a northern dialect word for a hill summit) which crest the great ridge dividing Lancashire and Yorkshire. The summit, at the end of a long but not difficult climb, gives you a glorious viewpoint in both directions, so save this ride for a clear day when the views can be fully enjoyed.

Gisburn Forest and Stocks Reservoir

Stocks Reservoir, like Gisburn Forest, is man-made but nevertheless provides a fine landscape feature. There are picnic areas near the reservoir and in the largely coniferous forest, and a choice of waymarked off-road mountain bike cycle trails through the woodland, making this a pleasant point to stop.

Slaidburn

This beautifully situated village in the upper Hodder Valley lies in spectacular open fell country, seen to great advantage on the steep descent from

Below: The war memorial at the crossroads in Slaidburn.

Gisburn Forest. It has few equals in the northwest of England for both character and charm. There is a pretty bridge over the River Hodder, a large village green, a popular cyclists' and walkers' café, a village shop and the celebrated Hark to Bounty Inn, a fine 18th-century hostelry with a splendid sign. There is also a youth hostel in the village for anyone wishing to break his or her journey with an overnight stay.

Cross of Greet Pass

This moorland pass, which follows the River Hodder almost to its source on Whiteray Fell, is steeper and tougher (with some lost height which has to be regained) than Bowland Knotts, rising to 427m. It goes through a landscape of desolate beauty which has much in common with the Scottish Highlands, starting from the isolated Cross of Greet Bridge and rising to the summit of the pass which is marked by the base of the ancient medieval Cross of Greet, which was once the boundary between Yorkshire and Lancashire when Slaidburn and the upper Hodder Valley were part of the old West Riding. During the long descent into the Wenning Valley, over Lythe and Tatham Fells, there are superb views across to the coast at Morecambe Bay.

Starting Point: Bentham station, in High Bentham, on the railway from Lancaster to Skipton and Leeds. There is adequate parking in the village. Alternatively, this ride can start and finish in Slaidburn — there is a good car park in the village.

Finishing/Return Point: Bentham station.

Distance: 48km (30 miles).

Time: 5 hours.

Map: OS Landranger 103: Blackburn & Burnley.

Surfaces and Gradients: There are good surfaces throughout. In terms of gradients, this is a very hilly, strenuous ride with few level stretches, even before the two main moorland passes. Suitable low gears are required, don't rush at the climbs and don't be ashamed of walking the steepest sections. Care is also required on the long descents which can have sharp bends — often with farm traffic coming in the opposite direction at critical points.

Traffic Conditions: Both the two main moorland passes and linking roads are generally quiet, with the possible exception of the B6478 into Slaidburn which can have busy traffic at weekends.

Facilities:
Cafés: Bentham, Slaidburn.
Pubs: Bentham, Slaidburn.
Shops: Bentham, Slaidburn.
WCs: Bentham, Slaidburn.
Youth Hostels: Slaidburn, Ingleton.

Left: The summit of Cross of Greet Pass.

Below: A wayside chapel near Stocks Reservoir.

ROUTE INSTRUCTIONS:

From Bentham station entrance (either platform) turn right at the end of the station drive and go down past Bentham's Victorian church to Bentham Bridge. Turn sharp left once you are over the bridge to go along an unmarked lane which follows the River Wenning, before climbing quite steeply past a farm to join Mewith Lane. Turn left again along another pleasant undulating lane, soon enjoying increasingly fine views left across to Ingleborough and its limestone pavements, and gradually ascend beyond Brown Bank Gill to Mewith Head. Keep ahead to climb to the cross-roads joining Keasden Road, the main lane from Clapham village.

Turn right and start the steady ascent past a series of moorland farms. The long Keasden Road heads due south and gradually rises up the fellside, soon crossing open heather moorland with lines of grouse butts, the road getting gradually steeper as it approaches the summit with its cattle grid and line of crags. This is a good place for rest and refreshment before a fairly hair-raising descent (care needed!) down the fellside, curving round and down towards Gisburn Forest directly ahead, with a steep drop into the valley of Hasgill Beck, then climbing back up the other side and through the forest. The road now goes round

the shore of Stocks Reservoir, climbing past a little chapel before the ascent to the main B6478 at Stephen Moor. Turn right here; the road climbs for another 40m to the summit before a steep descent into Slaidburn, with a particularly acute and steep bend near Whiteholme that must be negotiated with care. You arrive in the centre of Slaidburn by the village green, with toilets, car park and café nearby.

Most people will stay to enjoy a welcome break and refreshments in Slaidburn. The route back to Bentham starts at the crossroads by the war memorial, the narrow road heading north up and over a series of punishing low hills above Stocks Reservoir, before the more serious climbing starts beyond Cross of Greet Bridge which crosses the little River Hodder that feeds Stocks Reservoir. This is a tough, long climb, which becomes steeper as the summit approaches, following the narrow valley of the River Hodder before the last, severe ascent to Greet Cross — another place to rest in order to catch your breath and enjoy a great view.

There now follows an exhilarating descent, with long, open views spreading out before you. After the first steep descent, you lose height relatively gradually as the road follows the contours of Lythe Fell and switchbacks down to Crossdale Beck, from where some height has to be regained. Compared to earlier sections, this is easy going and you soon reach the junction with Mewith Lane, dropping down to Bentham Bridge then with a final pull up to High Bentham with its welcoming pubs, cafés and railway station.

ROUTE 9
BOWLAND KNOTTS

Rail to Carnforth, Lancaster ←

HIGH BENTHAM Stn

Rail to Skipton, Leeds →

Clapham Stn

KEASDEN

MEWITH HEAD

BOWLAND KNOTTS

CROSS OF GREET

R. Hodder

Gisburn Forest

Stocks Resvr.

SLAIDBURN

N ↑

Above: The Hark to Bounty Inn sign, Slaidburn.

A PENDLE MEANDER: NELSON TO WHALLEY

This ride explores some of Pendle's loveliest countryside, mostly within the Forest of Bowland Area of Outstanding Natural Beauty. It has a hilly start on the approach to Barley and then climbs over the shoulder of Pendle Hill, where you will be rewarded by fine views. Descending to the Ribble Valley, the ride follows undulating lanes through villages in the shadow of Pendle Hill, ending at Whalley with its famous Cistercian abbey.

BACKGROUND AND PLACES OF INTEREST:

Pendle Hill

Pendle Hill, the 532m-high gritstone outlier of the Pennines whose long whaleback shape dominates this ride and gives its name to Pendle District, is one of Lancashire's most famous landmarks and viewpoints. It is also rich in history, being the site of one of the chain of beacons which were lit to bring news of major national events such as the Spanish Armada, and also has associations with the Pendle Witches of romantic novel fame.

Barley

Barley is, with Downham, the most popular tourist village within Pendle. It has an attractive main street, a choice of cafés and pubs, a picnic area and a small information centre. Its popularity stems from its close proximity to Pendle Hill, being a popular place to start a walk to the summit of the beacon, but it is also a favourite calling point for cyclists enjoying a ride around the area.

Downham

One of the prettiest villages in Lancashire, Downham, on Pendleside, is beautifully preserved, with a green and a winding stream. Most of the properties belong to the Downham Estate, owned by the Assheton family of Downham Hall, whose coat of arms emblazon the village inn. The village toilets in the old stables at the bottom of the village (discreetly signed) are reputedly the prettiest in Lancashire.

Waddington

The village, named after a Saxon leader Wada, earned a small footnote in history when the Lancastrian Henry VI took refuge in Waddington Old Hall during the Wars of the Roses. He was discovered by Yorkist sympathisers, escaped but was recaptured in Clitheroe Woods. The village is also known for its superb Coronation Gardens in the centre, and has some attractive almshouses on the green.

Whalley

This is one of the most attractive small towns in the Ribble Valley, with rows of Tudor and Georgian cottages and shops along its main street, but what really makes Whalley special are the gaunt ruins of Whalley Abbey, a once-important Cistercian monastery. This was established on the banks of the Ribble in 1296 when Abbot Gregory of Norbury arrived with 20 monks. The monastery soon prospered, expanding rapidly during the 14th century. There is now a visitor centre with an exhibition in the abbey grounds. Also worth seeing (and travelling over) is the 49-arch brick viaduct which makes a dramatic feature above the town as it carries the Ribble Valley railway line across the river.

Left: A courtyard in Barley.

Starting Point: Nelson station. There are hourly trains on the East Lancashire line from Burnley, Blackburn and Preston. Motorists are advised to park in Blackburn and take the outward train to Nelson, returning from Whalley.

Finishing/Return Point: Whalley. There are hourly trains on the Ribble Valley line to Blackburn, Bolton and Manchester.

Distance: 29km (18 miles).

Time: $3^1/_2$ hours.

Map: OS Landranger 103: Blackburn & Burnley.

Surfaces and Gradients: There is one short 300m section of stony path along an old road out of Carr Hall; otherwise the route is on tarmac lanes. The first half of the ride is hilly and fairly strenuous, but after Downham it is on easy terrain.

Traffic Conditions: Traffic is generally moderate, but can be quite busy on Sunday afternoons because of visitor traffic in the Pendle Hill area.

Facilities:
Cafés: Nelson, Barley, Downham, Chatburn, Waddington, Whalley.
Pubs: Nelson, Barley, Downham, Chatburn, West Bradford.
Shops: Nelson, Barley, Downham, Chatburn, Waddington, Whalley.
WCs: Barley, Downham, Waddington, Whalley.
Tourist Information: Nelson, Barley.

ROUTE INSTRUCTIONS:

From Nelson station entrance keep to the left and cross the car park, going straight ahead at the cross-roads to pass the side of the Station Hotel. Turn left on to Broadway then go straight ahead at the traffic lights. Follow the road down the hill, over the canal and down under the motorway. At the bottom of the hill, just by the park, turn left after the bridge on to Park Avenue.

Follow Park Avenue to the end of the road. Cross the main road to Carr Hall Road, up the hill. At the next crossroads take Sand Hall Road, staggered slightly to the right. This narrow lane ends at a path. Go through the gate and continue to the summit of the path (as this is a footpath, cyclists should walk).

When you reach the road, turn right to descend steeply. Go straight ahead at the next junction and follow the road to Barley village. From Barley turn right to follow the lane up the side of Pendle Hill.

The road soon descends (with wide views across into Ribblesdale and the Yorkshire Dales); take the next left at the cross-roads, to descend to Downham.

In Downham, cross the bridge as the road climbs a short, steep slope through the village. Continue on this road as it descends again to Chatburn, keeping on it until it ends at a T-junction. Turn left and take the next right just after the dip in the road, signed for Grindleton. Follow Ribble Lane as it descends to the River Ribble and at the next T-junction turn left for Waddington.

Below: The view to Barley and Nelson from Pendle Hill.

Above: Downham village.

This lane follows the Ribble, passing through West Bradford before emerging at Waddington. Take the left fork just before the main junction down to the crossroads. Go straight ahead on the road signed for Mishill, and follow it as it winds out of the village, ignoring the turn-off left. Continue along the lane until the next junction; turn left then immediately right on the road signed for Longridge. After 750m (½ mile) turn left.

Turn right on to the B6243 and follow this to Great Mitton. As the main road bends sharply right, continue straight ahead. Turn left when this meets the main road at the edge of the hamlet and continue on this road over the Ribble and into Whalley.

Whalley station is immediately after the railway viaduct on this road on the left. For Whalley town centre continue straight ahead, or if you just want to catch sight of the abbey, before your train, turn right just before the viaduct as the lane passes the abbey via the impressive northwest gateway.

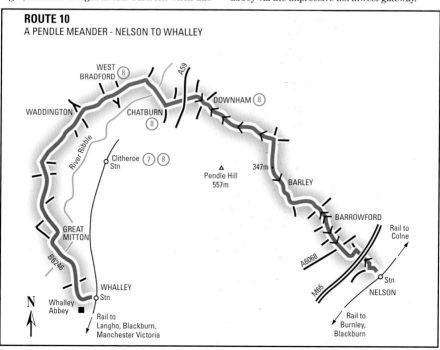

ROUTE 10
A PENDLE MEANDER - NELSON TO WHALLEY

THE LONG CAUSEWAY: BURNLEY TO HEBDEN BRIDGE

Starting in Burnley, Lancashire, and ending in Hebden Bridge, West Yorkshire, this trans-Pennine ride follows an ancient moorland route which crosses above Cliviger Gorge, one of the most dramatic passes of the South Pennines. There is much of interest along this route (it could easily be combined with a visit to Towneey Hall and Heptonstall's old church) and, in clear weather, there are some panoramic views, especially across Upper Calderdale.

BACKGROUND AND PLACES OF INTEREST:

Burnley

Burnley may be a busy industrial town, being the former centre of the cotton industry, but it is also rich in places of heritage interest. Most notable is The Weavers' Triangle, comprising a cluster of cottages and mills, a restored canal warehouse (complete with the Navigation Wharf pub), a café and a heritage centre with restored school rooms. Close by is The Straight Mile, a huge stone viaduct 20m above the town, on which the Leeds-Liverpool Canal is carried.

Towneley Hall Art Gallery and Museum

Set in beautiful woodland and gardens, Towneley Hall was the home of the Towneley family from the 15th century until 1902. The house has a wonderful Elizabethan long gallery, a collection of furniture and Royal Lancashire Pottery, an exhibition of local crafts and industries and a Natural History Centre. It is open daily (except Mondays) all year. The park and gardens are also open to the public and there is a café.

Hurstwood

It is worth making the 2km (1 mile) detour to Hurstwood to see this village in the upper Burn Valley, with its cluster of Tudor and Elizabethan houses. These include Hurstwood Hall, a fine yeoman's house built by Barnard Towneley in 1579, and Spenser's Cottage, which was reputedly the home from 1576-9 of Edmund Spenser

(1522-99), the great Elizabethan poet who wrote *The Faerie Queene*. Though the village has grown in recent years, with new housing development, its charm remains. At the far side of the village, where the cul-de-sac road ends, is a small car park and picnic area, with walks round Hurstwood Reservoir — source of the little River Burn that gives Burnley its name. Sadly, cyclists are not permitted to use the tracks which extend across the surrounding moorland.

The Long Causeway

The moorland road which runs along the crest of the hillside from Mereclough to Heptonstall, above Cliviger Gorge, is one of the most ancient routes in the Pennines. It was originally a prehistoric ridgeway and an important trade route, perhaps dating back to Bronze Age times when the valleys were filled with impenetrable scrub and swamp. It also formed part of the packhorseway used by medieval clothiers and merchants between Burnley and Halifax, with a causeway of grit flagstones to assist horses across the soft peat — hence the name Long Causeway. To guide travellers over the lonely moors, wayside crosses were erected. The site of one of these, Maiden Cross, with a carved inscription stone can still be seen in the wall close to the huge wind farm which makes such a dramatic, if intrusive, feature on the summit of the ancient moorland pass. There are panoramic views across the South Pennine Moors, and into Upper Calderdale, along the entire length of the road.

Heptonstall

Perhaps the finest example in the Pennines of a hill village, more characteristic of the Mediterranean than northern parts of Europe. This was a typical weavers' settlement, where hand-loom weaving (together with sheep rearing) was a vital part of the Pennine economy. There are many interesting buildings in the village; none more so than the ruined medieval church, abandoned in the middle of the 19th century and now making a melancholy ruin, with many remarkable gravestones around it. The old grammar school by the church is now a small museum which is open at weekends.

Hebden Bridge

Often described as the capital of the South Pennines, Hebden Bridge is noted for the curious four-storey 'double' houses that cling in narrow terraces to the steep hillsides, and for its many textile mills, often now converted to other uses. There is a choice of cafés and pubs, a pleasant canalside park and the perfectly preserved Lancashire & Yorkshire Railway station with a recently reopened buffet.

Left: Towneley Hall.

Above: Coal Clough wind farm, Cliviger Gorge.

Starting Point: Burnley Barracks station, on the East Lancashire railway line between Preston and Colne. If you are coming from Blackpool, or anywhere in West Yorkshire, and use one of the Trans-Pennine express trains to Burnley Manchester Road, you can join the route at the Weavers' Triangle, reached just off Manchester Road below the traffic island. There is a choice of official car parks in Burnley close to the canal cycleway.

Finishing/Return Point: Hebden Bridge station. Trains run hourly on weekdays and two-hourly on Sundays between Hebden Bridge and Burnley Manchester Road.

Distance: 29km (18 miles).

Time: 3¾ hours.

Map: OS Landranger 103: Blackburn & Burnley.

Surfaces and Gradients: There are good surfaces throughout, except for the short sections of canal towpath which is a perfectly adequate dirt track but take care on the flagstones and cobblestones past the Navigation Wharf Inn. Gradients start reasonably easily, but there are some quite stiff climbs out of the Calder and Burn valleys, as well as through Colden and through Mereclough, on a tight bend where walking is advised. This is more than compensated for by some thrilling descents, though care is required at times, such as downhill from Heptonstall.

Traffic Conditions: Traffic is generally reasonable, although there are short sections on busy roads in both Burnley and Hebden Bridge. On weekends Townley Park can be busy, and there can be more than enough motorists also enjoying the fine views along the Long Causeway on Sunday afternoons.

Facilities:
Cafés: Burnley, Townley Park, Hebden Bridge.
Pubs: Burnley (Weavers' Triangle), Mereclough, Hawks Stones (Sportsman's Arms on Long Causeway), Blackshaw Head, Colden, Heptonstall, Hebden Bridge.
Shops: Burnley, Hebden Bridge.
WCs: Burnley, Hebden Bridge.
Tourist Information: Burnley, Hebden Bridge.
Youth Hostel: Mankinholes near Todmorden.

ROUTE INSTRUCTIONS:
From Burnley Barracks station entrance follow the cycleway to the left along the markings which allow cyclists to ride along the pavement. Bypass the traffic lights and go down to the left where the entrance to the Canal Cycleway is indicated. Keep left under the bridge and follow the cycleway, soon reaching the paved section of path under the great warehouse canopy and the welcoming Navigation Wharf Inn at the Weavers' Triangle.

(The alternative starting point is Manchester Road station. Turn left outside the station on Manchester Road, going round the traffic island towards the town centre but, as you cross the canal bridge to reach the Weavers' Triangle, cross the road carefully to where you will see, at the far side, a sloping entry point on to the Canal Cycleway. Turn left here.)

Continue along the cyclepath for around 400m, going under the inner ring road, and eventually you reach another exit point at Finsley Gate just before the Straight Mile Viaduct (you may wish to go some way along the Straight Mile — actually only ¾ mile long — to enjoy the superb views across the roofscapes of the town). Otherwise, enter Parliament Street, turning left down to the small traffic island, and keep left as it descends to another island, this time on the A614 road. Turn right past the pedestrian entrance to Towneley Park but then take the next left along the park drive — a quiet, tree-lined avenue. If you plan to visit the park or the hall, keep straight ahead at the fork, otherwise follow the drive left as it curves behind the park. At the cross-roads just past the overflow car park, and before the garden centre, turn left to climb the long rear drive past the deer pond. At the summit of the hill, a cycle gate allows access on to a residential street which curves left. Go right at the T-junction and right again on the main road which climbs out of Burnley's outer suburbs towards Mereclough.

At the next road junction turn left along the lane down towards Worsthorne, then right at the next junction with the Hurstwood signs, eventually descending to the village in the Burn valley with its cluster of Elizabethan houses and, directly behind the village, the picnic area.

Retrace the route back to the main road to Mereclough — a steep ascent. Turn left, continuing on to the village of Mereclough; the road turns sharp left in the village, signed Blackshaw Head and Heptonstall. This is an extremely steep, curving road (walking is advised), the gradient of which eventually becomes more level, although still a steady climb, with ever more impressive views as you climb. At the summit by the wind farm there is a small car park. Directly opposite in the wall is the Maiden Cross stone — probably not the original cross but marking its position.

Follow Long Causeway as it skirts the moorland past the superbly positioned Stiperden Bar House, and cross the boundary of West Yorkshire, alongside Stansfield Moor. The road curves westwards past the isolated Sportsman's Arms pub and the junction with the road to Todmorden (no train service back to Burnley from here). Keep ahead and gently descend to the moorland village of Blackshaw Head. Keep left at the junction, heading for Heptonstall, go down a steep hill through the village of Colden and cross Colden Water beck, with the last steep climb of the day back up to the scattered hamlet of Slack. At the junction take the 'Heptonstall Only' road on the right. Take time to explore this superb moorland village with its cobbled main street. Keep directly ahead downhill (cars are discouraged but bikes are OK), taking care at the next very steep junction where the lane filters into the main motor route to Hebden Bridge. Go down the steep hill to the traffic lights which are at such an acute angle that no left turn for motor vehicles is permitted (cyclists don't have a problem). Follow the main A646 into Hebden Bridge town centre at the

traffic lights. For the station, keep on the main road for some 400m beyond the lights where the red Metro sign on the right indicates the station drive, at the top of which is the superbly preserved Victorian station.

Opposite: The ruined nave of Heptonstall's medieval church.

Below: The Maiden Cross on the Long Causeway.

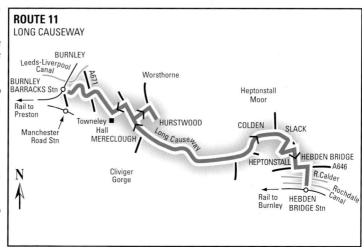

ROUTE 11
LONG CAUSEWAY

N

SUNDERLAND POINT AND HEYSHAM VILLAGE: MORECAMBE CIRCULAR

Taking advantage of the popular Morecambe-Lancaster cycleway, this easy ride follows the Lune estuary across the tidal road to the atmospheric village of Sunderland on the edge of the peninsula, using a bridlepath and back lanes to take in Heysham's historic church before returning along the seafront to Morecambe.

BACKGROUND AND PLACES OF INTEREST:

Morecambe
This popular seaside resort has, in recent years, reinvented itself, with a fine new promenade and the restored Stone Jetty filled with sculptures and reliefs of sea birds as part of the Tern Public Art Project, as well as the delightful dancing statue of the late Eric Morecambe by sculptor Graham Ibbetson which takes full advantage of a superb setting across Morecambe Bay, encircled by the Lakeland hills. As with any seaside resort, the town has every possible facility, but sadly is not all that cycle-friendly, with by-laws prohibiting cycling along the wide promenades, even on the higher level terraces on the Heysham side of the town.

Morecambe-Lancaster Cycleway
This popular 5km-long (3-mile) cyclepath and walkway follows the line of the old Lancaster-Green Ayre-Morecambe electric railway which was closed by the Beeching axe in the 1960s.

Overton
A pleasant village with a small, ancient church with a Norman nave, overlooking the Lune near Bazil Point, and two inns. In 1650 the village people petitioned for their own parson because they were cut off by the tides twice a day — something that still happens to nearby Sunderland.

Sunderland
Sunderland can only be reached by road over a low stretch of lane below the surrounding salt marshes, which is covered by high tides and is usually full of wet mud and sand so care is required. A warning notice at the edge of the marsh warns drivers — and cyclists — not to proceed if the posts supporting the notice are already under water. It is sensible to check locally

the times of tides before leaving Overton. Astonishing as it seems now, in the early 18th century the hamlet was once a busy transatlantic port for both the cotton and the slave trade, and it is claimed the first bale of cotton ever landed in England was in Sunderland. It was also important for shipbuilding and between 1715 and 1730 10 seagoing ships were constructed here. Much of the trade transferred to the improved docks in Lancaster in the later part of the century, and to Glasson Dock across the Lune which was linked to Lancaster by canal and later the railway (Route 13). Silting of the estuary and use of larger steam-powered ships needing the bigger harbours at the competing ports of Liverpool, Fleetwood and Heysham turned Sunderland into a forgotten backwater by the early 19th century, even though it enjoyed a short period as a Regency seabathing resort before being overtaken by its bigger, rail-served rival, Morecambe.

Sambo's Grave
Sambo was a little black boy, a captain's servant who came to Sunderland with his master in 1736 where he probably contracted a fever, dying in the house still known as Upsteps Cottage. Because he had not been christened he could not be buried in consecrated ground and his little grave is on the edge of a field on the other side of the peninsula, on which fresh flowers appear almost every day.

Starting Point: Morecambe station, on the branch railway from Lancaster. There are frequent trains from Lancaster, plus through services from Manchester, Preston, Leeds and Skipton. There is plenty of car parking nearby.

Finishing/Return Point: Morecambe station.

Distance: 23km (14 miles).

Time: 3 hours

Maps: OS Landranger 97: Kendal & Morecambe; 102: Preston & Blackpool.

Surfaces and Gradients: This route has a real mixture, ranging from the pleasant tarmac-surfaced Morecambe-Lancaster cycleway, minor roads and the causeway (often partially covered with sand and mud) to Sunderland, about 2km (1¹/₄ miles) of unsurfaced bridlepath where a mountain bike would be useful, country lanes and some sections of unavoidable main road back into Heysham and central Morecambe. The gradients are easy throughout with the exception of a couple of short, steep sections around Heaton and out of Heysham.

Heysham
The busy harbour, with its container port and ferry terminal and its attendant lorry traffic, and with the nuclear power station that dominates the skyline, are places to be avoided by cyclists, but the old village centre in Lower Heysham is totally unspoiled, with narrow streets, alleyways, old cottages, shops (some selling nettle beer) and cafés. Not to be missed are the ruins of the remarkable St Patrick's Chapel, an 8th century Saxon church with a carved grave in the bedrock. This is the oldest religious building in northwest England, and stands on a beautiful headland owned and managed by the National Trust. The nearby St Peter's Church is almost as venerable, dating from later Saxon times, with much Norman work as well as Viking hog-backed gravestones.

Traffic Conditions: Most of the main roads are quiet, and the cyclepath and bridlepath are traffic free. The short section of the A589 and the final stretch along Heysham Road (A5105) into Morecambe are busy, and care is required.

Facilities:
Cafés: Morecambe, Heysham.
Pubs: Morecambe, Golden Ball (Oxcliffe Hill), Overton, Middleton, Heysham.
Shops: Morecambe, Overton, Heysham.
WCs: Morecambe, Middleton, Heysham.
Tourist Information: Morecambe.
(NB: there are no facilities in Sunderland.)

Above left: Sunderland Point.

Left: Cyclists on the Morecambe–Lancaster Cycleway.

ROUTE INSTRUCTIONS:

From Morecambe station turn sharp left at the first traffic island and sharp left again at the next island in front of Morrison's supermarket, looking for the start of the cycleway on the left which is marked by a large relief shape of a cycle.

Follow the cycle trail, which is extremely well waymarked (keep to the cycle part of the trail), going alongside the main railway line before crossing the branch line to Heysham at a level crossing through the gates, then going through and along the back of a housing estate. Follow the trail for about 3km (2 miles), going under three road bridges, past the turn-off marked to White Lund and then between arching trees. At a junction of the ways, with a grassy area to the right, there is an entrance into a car park at the Salt Ayre sports and leisure complex. Turn right through the car park and go past the entrance gates, to where the path joins the busy A5273, a new road now filled with container trucks heading for Heysham harbour.

Mercifully, after a couple of hundred metres, you reach a traffic island. Ignore the signs to Overton and keep straight ahead following the signs to the Golden Ball Inn. This pleasant, quiet road which follows the sandy reed-covered banks of the River Lune, with fine views, then passes Oxcliffe Hill Farm and the Golden Ball Inn before joining a busier road towards Overton. At the next junction keep slightly left along an unmarked road down to Heaton Bottom, turning right at the bottom of the hill to go up a surprisingly steep gradient to rejoin the Overton road. Turn left at the next junction following the Overton signs, continuing ahead to the village of Overton now in view.

Above: The causeway to Sunderland Point with warning signs.

Unless you are going to view the church in Overton (reached by turning left along a cul-de-sac lane at the junction in the village centre), keep ahead past both inns towards Sunderland. This soon descends and crosses open salt marsh by the Lune estuary on a remarkable tidal road with a large red warning notice to be taken very seriously if the tide is coming in.

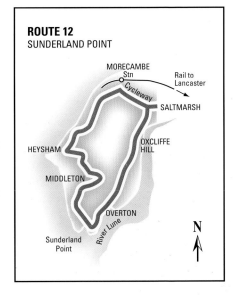

ROUTE 12
SUNDERLAND POINT

Follow the road — noting boats worryingly on either side of the road — to the hamlet of Sunderland. The public road ends by a tall stone post, but the little track which goes off to the right past Upsteps Cottage, known as The Lane, is a public bridlepath and, though narrow, is perfectly cycleable (give way to pedestrians). This reaches the foreshore on the Morecambe Bay side at a gate. For Sambo's Grave, dismount and walk for around 120m to where a stile on the left gives access to the little grave with its decorative stones and fresh flowers.

Return to the bridlepath, this time following the increasingly rough, sandy and stony track (where it is more sensible to walk) for some 500m to where it joins a good stony track which bears left across the foreshore to Potts Corner, where the tarmac starts. Follow this lane as it zigzags past farms whose principal crop seems to be caravan sites, with the huge bulk of Heysham nuclear power station ahead. The road winds its way through Middleton village and joins a busier road heading towards Heysham. Descend to a large traffic island, crossing at the all-too-short cycleway

crossings, then keep ahead up the A589 Middleton Road towards Heysham Village and Morecambe. At a fork in the road keep ahead on the quieter road, which becomes Smithy Lane, straight past the post office. Where this bears right to rejoin the main Morecambe road, turn left along School Road which soon descends to a junction. Go left here down Crime Well Lane, bearing right along Main Street into the centre of Heysham. St Peter's Church and St Patrick's Chapel lie up a steep lane (pedestrians only) to the left.

The return to Morecambe lies along the one-way system in Bailey Lane, turning left to climb up Knowlys Road to rejoin the main Heysham Road. Turn left here for the 3km (2-mile) ride to Morecambe seafront and town centre, though you may be tempted to turn left at the traffic lights on Whinnysty Lane to follow back roads or even the cliff-top path above the promenade into the town centre.

Below: St Patrick's Chapel, Heysham.

Above: A view across the Lune estuary towards Sunderland Point, from the shore near Crook Cottages.

GLASSON DOCK AND COCKERSAND ABBEY: LANCASTER CIRCULAR

This fairly easy circular ride from Lancaster takes advantage of the popular Glasson Dock cycleway down to the mouth of the Lune estuary, exploring this port which is still working, before taking quiet back lanes to enjoy more views of the estuary and the surviving fragment of Cockersand Abbey. The return route follows quiet lanes to enter Lancaster alongside the picturesque Lancaster Canal.

BACKGROUND AND PLACES OF INTEREST:

Lancaster

Spend time before or at the end of the cycle ride to explore Lancaster, one of England's most fascinating cities. This ancient seaport has a castle and priory (parish) church dating from the 14th century, the Maritime Museum, quayside areas with impressive warehouses, the 18th century Judge's Lodgings, a market and a pedestrianised centre. Take care with the incessant, heavy traffic which gridlocks the city centre.

Glasson Dock

Glasson developed into a busy port at the end of the 18th century when the silting of the river made Lancaster impossible to reach by the ever larger ocean-going merchant ships, which could easily anchor at Glasson's natural tidal basin. Trade peaked in the early 19th century with vessels heading as far away as the West Indies. It was linked to Lancaster by a branch of the Lancaster Canal from Galgate in 1826 to allow the trans-shipment of goods, and by railway in 1887. The impressive canal basin and locks still remain, now filled with leisure craft. Still a working harbour, the old port with its quaysides, three old inns, cafés and riverside views remains a hive of activity and a popular local visitor attraction.

The Glasson Dock Cyclepath

The old railway line between Lancaster and Glasson Dock was built in 1887 to serve what was then a thriving port on the Lune estuary, with a station at Conder Green where there is now a picnic site. Services were an early victim of road competition and the line closed to passengers in 1930 and to freight in 1947. The trackbed was acquired by Lancashire County Council in 1970 and it was converted into a cycleway. There is a pleasant picnic area near the end of the cycleway, before the bridge into Glasson Dock, with a refreshment van usually parked there at weekends.

The Lune Estuary

There are fine views across the Lune estuary from various points along this ride. The estuary, once an important commercial waterway, is now a Site of Special Scientific Interest, noted as a haven for a wide variety of birdlife including redshank, mallard, widgeon and shelduck as well as several rare plants and grasses.

Cockersand Abbey

The little octagonal building visible from the end of the public road is the surviving chapter house of the Abbey of St Mary of the Marsh of Cockersand. In 1080, Hugh Garth, a recluse and hermit, built his hermitage here. The land eventually passed to the monks of the Premonstratensian Order and despite once being extremely wealthy, with buildings that covered almost half a hectare, it has almost completely disappeared, its 14th century choir stalls now being in Lancaster's parish church. Only this unusual chapter house remains, and can be reached by public footpath which passes close by (no right to cycle). It is on private land and, being a family vault of the Dalton family, there is no public access to it.

The Lancaster Canal

Opened in sections from Preston to Wigan then to Lancaster and Kendal between 1797 and 1819, the original purpose of the canal was to transport coal from the Lancashire coalfields to north Lancashire and Westmorland. (It later linked with the Leeds-Liverpool Canal.) A major feature is the magnificent Lune Aqueduct crossing the River Lune north of Lancaster, designed by the great canal engineer John Rennie and opened in 1797. The branch to Glasson Dock, with its six locks, was opened in 1826. Though partly restored and popular as a leisure waterway, the building of the M6 severed the canal at Tewitfield, near Burton in Kendal, thus isolating the northern section. Current plans are for the eventual reopening of the whole canal.

Starting Point: Lancaster station. There are frequent train services from every part of Lancashire and Cumbria. There is adequate car parking in the city centre.

Finishing/Return Point: Lancaster station (circular).

Distance: 31km (19 miles).

Time: $3^1/_2$ hours.

Maps: OS Landranger 97: Kendal & Morecambe; 102: Preston & Blackpool.

Surfaces and Gradients: The Glasson Dock railway path runs 7km ($4^1/_3$ miles) on firm, cinder and earth track, otherwise there are good tarmac surfaces throughout. There are three short but steepish hills on the return sections towards and out of Galgate, and over Lunecliffe on the way into Lancaster.

Traffic Conditions: There is some urban traffic on the start out of Lancaster, and again into and leaving Glasson Dock. Minor roads in and out of Galgate and into Lancaster have some weekend rat-running traffic, otherwise it is fairly light.

Facilities:
Cafés: Lancaster, refreshment van at weekends at the picnic area on the end of the main cycleway near Glasson, Glasson Dock.
Pubs: Lancaster, Conder Green (the Stork Inn on the A588 400m from the end of the cycleway), Glasson Dock.
Shops: Lancaster, Glasson Dock.
WCs: Lancaster (station and town), Glasson at the end of the cycleway, Glasson Dock.
Tourist Information: Lancaster.

ROUTE INSTRUCTIONS:

From the rear entrance of Lancaster station (opposite the main Platform 3 for northbound trains) turn right into Station Road. Following the signs for Lune Industrial Estate, turn left into West Road, continue down Lune Road and go left at the river along New Quay Road. (New Quay was developed in 1767 to enable larger vessels to get closer to the city centre.) As the road seems to come to an end at a cluster of warehouses, keep ahead to where the Glasson Dock cycleway starts with a small sign indicating Glasson Dock $4^1/_2$

Above: Lancaster Castle. *North West Tourist Board*

Above: Glasson Dock.

miles. This begins with a pleasant tarmac track which soon gives way to a narrow ash and grass track between hedges. After a little less than 1km, where this narrows to a very narrow grassy path (often flooded), look for a gap on the left which leads on to the parallel line of the old railway. This level, well-drained cycleway soon reaches a junction of paths: ignore the cycleway on tarmac heading back into the south of the city; your way is ahead through the gate on a straight, pleasant path, still on the old railway trackbed. The path is lined by hedges and some benches, and soon provides fine views across the marshland to Overton and Sunderland Point.

The track ends at a small car park and picnic site. Keep ahead but rather than following the waymarked route left to Conder Green along National Cycle Route 6, fork right on the track through a gateway which leads to the bridge across the little River Conder. The route then swings towards Glasson Dock; bear right with the path to reach the main road into Glasson Dock.

Cross the harbour swing bridge with its traffic lights, go through the village, up Tithe Barn Hill then descending on the road as it curves left behind the canal basin, to join the lane to Turnham. Turn right here down a quiet lane

through low-lying fields, before reaching another T-junction at which you should turn right again, along a lovely winding, narrow road past farms. At the next T-junction take the road marked 'Single Track — No Turning' on the right which winds to the shore below Crook Cottages where there is a small, informal private car park, and views across to the small lighthouse which marks the entrance to the Lune estuary. On the left, on a low headland, is the octagonal form of what is left of Cockersand Abbey. There is no access by cycle but you can, if you choose, walk the few hundred metres along the Lancashire Coastal Footpath for a closer look at the surviving sandstone chapter house.

Return the way you came, back to the junction with the road from Tithe Barn Hill, crossing the Lancaster Canal, then joining the B5290 road east of Glasson Dock. Turn right here alongside the salt marshes of the Conder estuary to reach the A588. Turn left over the river bridge then immediately sharp right along a lane to Galgate with width restriction signs, winding between fields before climbing a steep hill. Take care on both the ascent and descent: local traffic from Galgate uses this very narrow road as a short cut.

As you enter Galgate, a rapidly growing outer dormitory suburb of both Lancaster and Preston, keep straight ahead as the road swings right by new housing to join the back lane which runs parallel with the electrified main railway line. Turn left here, immediately making a surprisingly steep ascent of Highland Hill, above the railway cutting. Follow this undulating road for a little under 2km (1 mile), and then take a narrow lane (unsigned) on the left, known as Tarnwater Lane. This is a beautiful, extremely narrow lane where, hopefully, you will not meet any traffic as passing is extremely difficult. This descends to the canal, curves up past Brantbeck and then makes a steep descent to rejoin the A588. Cross with care and turn right.

After about 800m of steady climbing along this busy main road take the first lane on the left (unsigned), by pylons, which soon leads round to the right around the little hill of Lunecliffe. Continue in the same direction at the next rather awkward junction (no signs); you will soon have fine views back across the Lune estuary to Heysham power station as you head northwards into the lush suburb of Aldcliffe. Descend to a very attractive canalside area and immediately under the railway bridge turn left into Brook Street which leads into the traffic-calmed Dallas Road. Keep to the left of the traffic humps for comfort, noting the cycleway right into the city centre along the High Street. Otherwise turn left along Meeting House Lane to the railway station.

Below: The view across the Lune estuary marshes towards Overton.

Bottom: Cyclist near Conder Green.

53

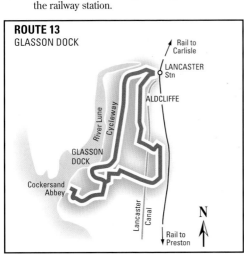

ROUTE 13
GLASSON DOCK

Rail to Carlisle

LANCASTER Stn

ALDCLIFFE

River Lune

Cycleway

GLASSON DOCK

Cockersand Abbey

Lancaster Canal

N

Rail to Preston

ARNSIDE AND SILVERDALE: CARNFORTH TO ARNSIDE

On the very edge of the Lake District, yet with a distinct character all of its own, the Arnside and Silverdale Area of Outstanding Natural Beauty shares its allegiance between Cumbria and Lancashire. This ride starts in Lancashire at the busy road and rail junction of Carnforth, seeks out narrow lanes through the foothills of the Lake District then crosses into the limestone country of Silverdale, before heading northwards to Arnside along the dramatic Kent estuary in Cumbria. The ride can also be combined with a visit to the popular RSPB Reserve of Leighton Moss to make a full day's trip.

BACKGROUND AND PLACES OF INTEREST:

Arnside and Silverdale Area of Outstanding Natural Beauty

Overlooking Morecambe Bay, this is a protected landscape covering some 75sq km of low limestone hills, the craggy summit of Arnside Knott being just 159m (522ft) above sea level. Native woodland and wild flowers, low cliffs, drystone walls and salt marsh combine to create a land and seascape of rich and intimate beauty.

Arnside

Superbly situated along the banks of the Kent estuary, and sheltered by the bulk of Arnside Knott, the little resort of Arnside has a narrow seafront and tiny pier, but its dominating features are the great railway viaduct across the Kent estuary to Grange-over-Sands, and the superb backcloth of the Furness Fells beyond. The ruined Arnside Tower, passed on the route to the right as you make the final ascent by Arnside Knott, is a fine example of a fortified pele tower built in the 15th century to provide a place of refuge in times of frequent raids by marauding Scots.

Silverdale

It is the setting rather than the village itself which makes Silverdale so attractive. Away from the main village street and modest church, residential and holiday accommodation has expanded but it is screened by lovely woodland and dominated by splendid views across the bay.

Carnforth
For details see Route 15.

Borwick
The attractive village of Borwick is dominated by the huge walled gardens of Borwick Hall, a Tudor merchant's house with a fine Elizabethan front. The house is now an outdoor adventure and leisure centre operated by Lancashire County Council, with accommodation available. Priest Hutton close by is a quiet, unspoiled farming village.

Burton in Kendal
This once important coaching town was for centuries on the main road to Scotland, midway between Kendal and Lancaster, where horses were changed at the village inns. Now mercifully bypassed by the M6 motorway, but still busy enough, Burton retains much of its charm, with several fine Georgian houses. The four recesses in the 18th century market cross were once used for chaining up village wrongdoers in a very public place.

Leighton Moss Nature Reserve
One of the finest bird and nature reserves in the northwest, the 130-hectare RSPB reserve at Leighton Moss is an extensive area of marshland and pond in the heart of Arnside and Silverdale AONB noted for breeding bitterns and is one of the few strongholds of the wild otter. Over 200 species of birds, waders and ducks have been recorded. What is to be seen varies with the season, as do the wild flowers. An excellent visitor centre (admission fee payable) prepares the visitor for a walk around the public area with its specially designed viewing hides. There are toilets and a shop on the site.

Starting Point: Carnforth station, on the railway line between Lancaster and Barrow. There are frequent trains from Manchester, Bolton, Preston, Lancaster and Barrow, plus less regular services from Leeds and Skipton. There is plenty of car parking in the town centre.

Finishing/Return Point: Arnside station. A return can be made to Carnforth on the direct road via Silverdale station and Crag Foot or Warton (an extra 15km or 9 miles approximately) but there is a remarkable amount of heavy traffic along these minor roads, including quarry waggons, and the 12min train ride from Arnside to Carnforth is a much more pleasant option.

Distance: 29km (18 miles).

Time: 3 hours.

Map: OS Landranger 97: Kendal & Morecambe.

Surfaces and Gradients: Good surfaces throughout, though on some of the narrower lanes around Priest Hutton and Keer Holme, farmyard mud and manure can be a hazard. Gradients are generally moderate, though there are a couple of fairly sharp ascents near Priest Hutton and by Arnside Knott, near the end of the ride, and one long, very steep ascent from the River Keer up to Hutton Roof Crags.

Traffic Conditions: The first 100m along Carnforth's main street is dominated by heavy traffic (walking to the traffic lights is advised) but once across the A6 and left past the Shovel Inn the traffic disappears for most of the route, although inevitably both Silverdale and Arnside are busy with tourist and local traffic at weekends.

Left: A cyclist on a quiet lane near Priest Hutton.

Above: Arnside Viaduct, overlooking the Kent estuary.

Facilities:
Cafés: Carnforth, Silverdale, Arnside.
Pubs: Carnforth, Burton in Kendal, Silverdale, Arnside.
Shops: Carnforth, Burton in Kendal, Silverdale, Arnside.
WCs: Carnforth, Arnside.
Youth Hostel: Arnside.

ROUTE INSTRUCTIONS:

From Carnforth station entrance cross the car park to the junction at the bottom of Market Street, going up to the traffic lights on the A6. Cross straight ahead but at the junction by the Shovel Inn turn left along North Road, signed to Borwick. This road climbs past terraced houses and enters open countryside, soon going under the Carnforth-Skipton railway line, over the A601 motorway link road then under the M6. At the junction with the lane from Over Kellet, turn left past the two artificial lakes on the left. At the next junction (unsigned) turn right into the village of Borwick.

As you come to the village centre, by the entrance to Borwick Hall turn sharp left along the lane which heads to the north of the village and then go on to the village of Priest Hutton. Once into the village turn sharp right along a narrow, unmarked lane which climbs past a farm and winds its way between fields before swinging southwards to rejoin the main road from Borwick. Turn left here for a few metres but immediately over the railway bridge turn sharp left, signed to Docker and Keer Holme. This pleasant lane follows the embankment of the Skipton railway line for almost 2km (1¹/₄ miles) before turning

sharp right — ignore this turn and keep ahead along a narrow lane still alongside the railway which goes uphill, signed for Burton and Hutton Roof.

This soon crosses the railway line at Keer Holme, heading northeastwards under pylons to join another lane near Docker Hall. Turn sharp left along the lane towards Keer Side and go back under the pylons, before losing height sharply down to the wooded stream and stone bridge over the River Keer. Now follows the longest climb on the ride, a steep ascent out of the little valley which continues as far as the junction with the Burton-Hutton Roof Road. Turn left towards Burton, the highest point at 157m being just 2m lower than the summit of Arnside Knott. The road now descends through the wood. Check your speed around a steep bend to the right, and 100m beyond this bend a minor road leads off to the right. This descends through woods past the hamlet of Dalton to reach the northern edge of Burton in Kendal.

It is worth cycling 150m into the village centre with its attractive Georgian houses and two pubs (both selling food), returning to the crossing at Tanpit Lane. This descends and bears left to a junction with a delightful antique Westmorland County Council road sign to the long-defunct Burton & Holme railway station. Follow this road right as it goes over the motorway, through a low and narrow tunnel beneath the Lancaster Canal, then on to a second tunnel, this time under the electrified West Coast main line. Immediately beyond the railway tunnel go sharp left, parallel to the railway, along a lane which eventually ascends to a T-junction. Turn right here towards the very busy A6 road ahead. Cross directly ahead to ascend to the pretty village of Yealand Redmayne, bearing right at the T-junction in the village. Keep left at the next junction, signed to Silverdale and Leighton Moss. Now follows a beautiful road, under a cover of trees, which soon reaches and follows Leighton Moss on the left, its ponds, reedbeds and marshlands alive with birds. The car park is on the right, and the visitor centre on the left.

From Leighton Moss continue over the Barrow railway line, turning right past Silverdale station (where the ride can be terminated) and continuing to the next main junction by the car park for Eaves Wood (National Trust). Ignore the Arnside sign ahead but bear left for Silverdale. As you enter the village take the narrow road which forks right at the junction. This descends to the sea edge, with fine views across Morecambe Bay. The road, now signed for Arnside, curves round through Far

Above: The Arnside foreshore, looking towards Arnside Point.

Arnside with its caravan sites, and begins a gentle but progressively steeper ascent of Arnside Knott, the tree-covered hill to your left. As you climb, note the grey square ruin of Arnside Tower on the right, commanding what is a narrow pass between the two wooded hilltops. The road clings to the left of this pass, soon reaches a summit and almost immediately enters the outskirts of Arnside on a steep descent into the village.

Go directly along the little promenade with its shops, cafés and pubs, and some 120m beyond the end of the village is the little station (now the headquarters of the AONB countryside service). Allow time to carry your bike over the steep footbridge to the far platform for trains to Carnforth, Lancaster and places beyond.

ROUTE 14
ARNSIDE & SILVERDALE

River Kent

Rail to Barrow

ARNSIDE Stn

A6070

A6

BURTON-IN-KENDAL

Leighton Moss

SILVERDALE

Leighton Moss Stn

M6

PRIEST HUTTON

BORWICK

River Keer

CARNFORTH Stn

N

Rail to Lancaster

A6

THE LUNE VALLEY AND THE HOWGILLS: OXENHOLME TO CARNFORTH

This ride starts at the fringes of the Lakes along twisting narrow back lanes then climbs into the upper reaches of the Lune Valley at the western foot of the Howgills, on the edge of the Yorkshire Dales National Park. Following the River Lune downstream, the route runs through Sedbergh and the bottom of Dentdale before rejoining the Lune on its gentle progression southwards. The steep western scarp slope of the Pennines is marked by picturesque villages such as Barbon and Kirkby Lonsdale. You then enter Lancashire and pass through the rolling green countryside close to the Leeds-Carnforth railway with a backcloth of fine views towards Ingleborough and the Yorkshire Dales. The route ends in Carnforth, where the hills finally give way to the narrow strip of marshy coastline around Morecambe Bay.

BACKGROUND AND PLACES OF INTEREST:

The Howgills Fells

With their steep-sided, rounded grassy peaks, these distinctive conical hills make a spectacular outlier of the Yorkshire Dales National Park. Geologically speaking, however, they have more in common with the nearby Lake District mountains, being of hard Silurian and Ordovician slates.

Below: Sedbergh main street.

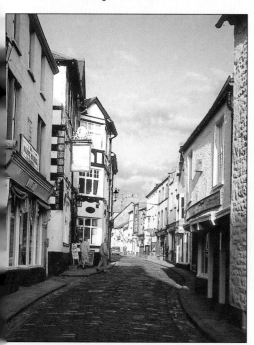

Sedbergh

A small Dales town, superbly situated under the Howgills, which forms the northwestern gateway into the Yorkshire Dales National Park, and the two Cumbrian dales of Garsdale and Dentdale. As well as its large public school, there are some interesting old weavers' cottages, the remains of a Norman motte and bailey castle and a medieval church. With its choice of shops, inns, cafés, and bed and breakfast establishments, this is a good base from which to explore the nearby Howgills and northwestern Dales. The Yorkshire Dales National Park has a visitor information centre on the main street.

Barbon

This small and attractive village with a Victorian church stands at the foot of Barbondale, one of the least known of the Yorkshire Dales. Barbondale follows a natural pass in the hills created by the great Pennine Fault which separates the characteristic Carboniferous limestone and gritstone rocks of the Yorkshire Dales from the older Ordovician and Silurian slates of the Lake District — hence the subtle change in the landscape as you travel southwards beyond the village.

Kirkby Lonsdale

Kirkby Lonsdale is a pleasant, mainly Georgian market town noted for its celebrated ancient bridge, fine church and famous viewpoint described by John Ruskin looking along the River Lune with a backcloth of fells beyond. Its position and choice of cafés make it a very popular stop-off point for motorists and cyclists travelling along the nearby A65 between West Yorkshire and the Lake District.

Carnforth

In the 19th century, Carnforth had a large haematite iron works, and it also developed as a major railway junction on the Furness & Midland Joint Railway, the station (now being restored) achieving fame as the setting for the restrained lovers in the classic film Brief Encounter. The pleasant main street, with its welcoming inn and cafés, and one of the best new and second-hand bookshops in the northwest, is blighted by incessant heavy traffic rat-running through the town centre to join the M6 near Warton.

Starting Point: Oxenholme railway station. There are frequent First North Western trains from Manchester, Bolton, Preston and Lancaster; regular Virgin West Coast/Cross Country trains (reservation fee for cycles) from Preston, Wigan and Carlisle. Motorists should park in Lancaster and take the outward train to Oxenholme.

Finishing/Return Point: Carnforth station. There are frequent trains to Lancaster, Preston, Barrow, Manchester, Skipton and Leeds.

Distance: 60km (38 miles).

Time: $5^1/_2$ hours.

Map: OS Landranger 97: Kendal & Morecambe.

Surfaces and Gradients: There are good tarmac surfaces throughout with some sharp, steepish hills, but without very long climbs.

Traffic Conditions: The route takes place on generally quiet roads and back lanes. Some care is required, however, with the heavy industrial traffic in Carnforth.

Facilities:
Cafés: Sedbergh, Kirkby Lonsdale, Carnforth.
Pubs: Oxenholme, Sedbergh, Barbon, Casterton, Kirkby Lonsdale, Whittington, Carnforth.
Shops: Sedbergh, Kirkby Lonsdale, Carnforth.
WCs: Sedbergh, Kirkby Lonsdale, Carnforth.
Tourist Information: Sedbergh, Kirkby Lonsdale.

ROUTE INSTRUCTIONS:
Exit from Oxenholme station, turn left on to the road and ascend the hill before dropping down the other side. Take the second left turn and then turn right. Follow the narrow lane, take the next right to go over the hillock and then turn left and left again on the road signed for New Hutton.

Go straight ahead across the A684 Sedbergh–Kendal road continuing with a gradual ascent. On the descent there is a junction near the base of the hill; go straight ahead where the road bends sharp left. Turn right at the bottom of the hill before the road regains height.

Follow the lane to the end and turn right. Take the road signed for Beckfoot at the next junction, crossing the M6 motorway, then take the next left after the motorway bridge as the road sweeps down to run parallel to the railway and motorway for a short distance. Continue along the lane as it narrows before a sharp drop into Beckfoot hamlet and the Lune Valley.

Turn right on to the B6257 towards Sedbergh, then left on to the A684. Follow the road straight ahead into the town centre, taking the one-way street ahead.

Leave Sedbergh by turning right at the end of the one-way street and then turn left at the roundabout. Take the Dent road, which drops down to cross the River Rawthey; as it climbs, turn right by the golf club sign. This lane narrows and

Below: Millthrop Bridge across the Rawthey, near Sedbergh.

crosses over a hump-backed bridge, and climbs again. The lane has a short unfenced section and so is gated. Passing Holme Open Farm, the lane bends sharp left to join the A683 after 1km (¾ mile). Continue straight ahead on the A683 and take the fifth left (about 5km/3 miles), or the second left after the Swan Inn, signed for Tossbeck Farm. Take the next right and follow this lane to the village of Barbon.

In Barbon turn left then right and continue along the lane, rejoining the A683 before the village of Casterton. As the road descends to the riverside, turn right to take the old bridge over the River Lune.

Go up the other bank and then turn right on to the A65, turning left immediately (turn right for Kirkby Lonsdale village). Following the Lune Valley as far as Newton turn right, take the road signed for Docker Park then the second right (signed Docker Park) to pass the show farm and follow it to the end. Turn right to go into Borwick. Turn left in the village, crossing over the Lancaster Canal before turning left at the crossroads. Take the next right to ascend again into Carnforth and turn right where you meet the B6254. Cross the A6 at the traffic lights to go straight ahead to Carnforth station which soon appears on your left.

Above: The Howgill Fells above Sedbergh.

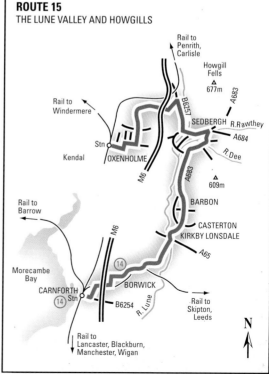

ROUTE 15
THE LUNE VALLEY AND HOWGILLS

THE COAL ROAD AND MALLERSTANG: DENT TO KIRKBY STEPHEN

This is a ride which will appeal to all railway enthusiasts. It follows the Settle–Carlisle line between Dent and Kirkby Stephen stations to reveal some of the most dramatic scenery along this rail corridor. The ride follows the ancient byway along the edge of Birkett Common with its limestone outcrops, and crosses the Pennine Fault into the red sandstone country of Eden, a geologically complex area not without its problems for railway builders and Railtrack to the present day because of frequent landslips. The ride can be combined with Route 18 from Kirkby Stephen to Appleby.

BACKGROUND AND PLACES OF INTEREST:

The Settle–Carlisle Railway Line

The Settle–Carlisle line is generally recognised to be England's most spectacular railway line because of its many dramatic engineering features and the superb views from the carriage window. The line was built between 1869 and 1875 and was the last major Victorian railway line to be built almost entirely by manual labour. It carried the Midland Railway's express trains between London St Pancras and Glasgow. After decades of neglect, the line was saved from closure by the efforts of thousands of protesters, and now has a regular local train service which gives access to the Yorkshire Dales National Park, the Eden Valley and the North Pennines AONB. This and the other recommended rides in the Eden Valley can be combined with a trip along the line.

Dent Station

At 331m or 1,150ft above sea level, Dent is the highest main line station in England. The station has been recently restored (although the main station building is privately owned and has no public access) and offers magnificent views from the station platforms down into Dentdale and the distant Howgill Fells. The stationmaster's house, on the right of the entrance drive, is reputed to have been the first house in England to be fitted with double-glazing because of the wild and windy climate. From the station it is a 7km (4^1/$_3$ mile) walk or ride to the lovely old town of Dent.

The Coal Road

The Coal Road takes its name from the shallow pits where, in days before railways and cheap transport, poor quality local coal was obtained to be sold in Dent and outlying settlements. The road also joins and combines with Galloway Gate, an ancient, broad moorland drove road where, until the Settle-Carlisle line was built, Scottish cattle were driven to markets in the English Midlands. Though it is a very steep climb from Dent station up Monkeybeck Grains (walking is advised), the views from the summit are superb, looking down Dentdale, across to the Three Peaks, the Howgill Fells and northwards into Garsdale and to Wild Boar Fell, soon passed on this ride.

Garsdale Station

This was once an important junction station, known as Hawes Junction, complete with glass canopies, a water tower, a turntable and a small engine shed. Here the North Eastern Railway Wensleydale line from Northallerton and Hawes joined the Midland Railway main line.

Aisgill and Mallerstang

Aisgill at 361m or 1,169ft above sea level is the summit of the Settle-Carlisle line and the watershed between the Ure and Eden river systems. It is worth visiting Hell Gill Force, a pretty waterfall reached by bridlepath (cycles permitted) through the gate just behind Aisgill Cottages. Aisgill is also the gateway to Mallerstangdale, a magnificent dale penetrated by a narrow road and the railway running between the impressive crags of Wild Boar Fell and Mallerstang Edge.

Pendragon Castle

The ruins of this little medieval castle, which once guarded the main entrance to the upper Eden Valley, occupy a strategic position with fine views of the surrounding hills. According to legend, the Celtic warrior prince Uther Pendragon, father of King Arthur, was born here.

Kirkby Stephen Station

Though not as gloriously situated as Dent, Kirkby Stephen station is another example of a rural Midland Railway station built in the standard so-called Derby Gothic style. It is now an important railhead and transport interchange for this area of rural Cumbria.

Above left: Railway cottages at Garsdale.

Left: The Coal Road

Starting Point: Dent station, on the Leeds-Settle-Carlisle railway line. Trains operate every two or three hours between Carlisle and Settle. It is advisable to book your cycle space on trains at busy times, including summer weekends — tel: 0845 7484 950 for information. There is no parking at Dent station but parking is available at Kirkby Stephen and Garsdale. Motorists are advised to park at Kirkby, take a suitable southbound train (usually less busy earlier in the day) and then cycle back to their vehicle. (Alternatively, the route can be shortened by 6km (3³/₄ miles) and steep gradients avoided by starting at Garsdale station.)

Finishing/Return Point: Kirkby Stephen station.

Distance: 25km (16 miles).

Time: 3 hours.

Maps: OS Landranger 91: Appleby; 98: Wensleydale & Wharfedale.

Surfaces and Gradients: The ride follows good tarmac roads with the exception of 3km (2 miles) between Pendragon Castle and Bullgill where a grass-and-stone-surfaced byway is used. There is an extremely steep gradient for the first 2km (1¹/₄ miles), but this is richly rewarded in good weather by some of the finest views in the Pennines. Once this is done, other gradients are fairly moderate, except for a short steep section at Bullgill near Kirkby Stephen.

Traffic Conditions: Most of the route is fairly quiet, though at weekends the short section of A684 between Garsdale station corner and The Moorcock can be busy. The 1km (¹/₂ mile) on the A685 to Kirkby Stephen station (downhill) is always busy and care should be taken, especially when crossing to the station entrance.

Facilities:
There are few facilities on this ride and you are advised to take supplies with you. Kirkby Stephen station is 2km (about 1¹/₄ miles) from the town centre it serves, but the return ride is not recommended because of the steep gradient and amount of very heavy industrial traffic on the A685 — weekends included.
Cafés: None.
Pubs: The Moorcock at Garsdale Head (A684/B6259 junction).
Shops: None.
WCs: None (limited facilities at Garsdale and Kirkby Stephen stations).
Youth Hostels: Denthead, Kirkby Stephen.

ROUTE INSTRUCTIONS:

From Dent station entrance turn sharp right uphill. This is an extremely steep climb (walking or very low gear recommended) for the 2km (1¹/₂ mile) ascent past Dodderham Moss plantation and up to Monkeybeck Grains, where the gradient eases as the Coal Road snakes its way over the summit ridge before the thrilling descent past Garsdale station. This is one of the highest roads and moorland passes in the Yorkshire Dales National Park, and is often closed in the winter with lying snow. (If there is snow on the hilltops, you are advised to alight at Garsdale station.)

Continue to the Coal Road's junction with the A684, turning right past the little chapel and under Dandry Mire viaduct to the Moorcock Inn, the only place of refreshment on this ride. Turn left along the B6259 following the Kirkby Stephen sign]. The now gently undulating road heads due north, passing under the railway at Shaw Paddock, gradually ascending to Aisgill Cottages, then descending gently to recross the railway into Mallerstang. Keep ahead past the hamlet of Outhgill with its little chapel, and go on to Pendragon where, at a junction, a narrow lane on the left winds its way below the castle and over a bridge across the River Eden. Where the lane turns sharp left and becomes unenclosed over Birkett Common, keep straight ahead along the grass and stone track which follows the riverside, swinging round past low hills before climbing up to rejoin a tarmac farm road near another ruined castle, Lammerside (accessible by field path). This lane now climbs steadily past Bullgill Farm with its isolated telephone kiosk, going under the railway line at Wharton Dikes farm and eventually joining the A683 just before its junction with the A685. A short ride through heavy traffic soon brings you to Kirkby Stephen station.

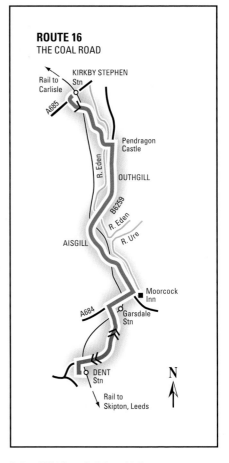

ROUTE 16
THE COAL ROAD

Below: Wild Boar Fell, from Mallerstang.

ACROSS THE STAINMORE GAP: KIRKBY STEPHEN CIRCULAR

This ride covers the higher part of the Eden and its tributary valleys surrounding Kirkby Stephen, skirting the edges of the Yorkshire Dales, the North Pennines and Crosby Garrett Fell. The route offers breathtaking views of the great escarpment wall of the North Pennines and, in the distance, the peaks of the Lake District. On the final leg of the ride there are impressive views looking southwards towards Nine Standards Rigg and Mallerstang, the northernmost part of the Yorkshire Dales (see Route 16), with a steady climb back to Kirkby Stephen station on the Settle–Carlisle Line.

BACKGROUND AND PLACES OF INTEREST:

Kirkby Stephen

This busy town, the name of which is thought to have originated from 'Kirkby vest Idun' meaning church town west of the Eden, is the unofficial capital of the upper Eden Valley. The town received its market charter in 1351 and still has a Monday market. It is strategically positioned at a cross-roads of still important highways which lead to Kendal, Tebay and Barnard Castle. Its many cafés, pubs and Georgian and early Victorian houses and shops bear witness to its role as a staging point in former times for horse-drawn traffic, and in more recent years for motor traffic between Teesside, Tyneside and the Lancashire coast. It has a small market place, and a particularly splendid parish church, which includes the famous Wharton Chapel, full of fascinating medieval carvings, fragments of Anglo-Saxon crosses, a Viking hog-backed gravestone and a rare carving of Logi the Anglo-Viking pagan fire god. There is an attractive riverside area behind the town.

Hartley

This village was once dominated by Harcla Castle, home to Sir Andrew de Harcla, who was a very significant figure during Edward II's reign. However, he was accused of treason and executed in 1325, his lands passing on to other lords. The hillsides near the village have a long history of quarrying —coal, copper and lead having been extracted in the past — and there is still a large limestone quarry above Hartley today.

Right: Brough Castle.

Stainmore

This great moorland pass across the Pennines between Brough and Bowes rises to over 400m and since Roman times has been a vital trans-Pennine artery, now carrying the main A66 road. Until the 1950s it also carried the railway line opened by the South Durham & Lancashire Union Railway in 1863. This ran from Barnard Castle to Kirkby Stephen, Appleby and Tebay and was built to carry Durham coke to the Cumbrian and north Lancashire ironworks. It was the highest standard gauge railway in England, requiring major engineering structures, including the long vanished Belah Viaduct near Kirkby Stephen. The line closed in 1962 but surviving sections to Hartley Quarry from Appleby remained in use until the 1980s, and to Warcop MOD base until the 1990s. A short section of track remains, hopefully eventually to be reopened as a preserved railway, between Appleby East station and Warcop.

Brough

Brough's 2,000-year-long history is intimately connected with the road over Stainmore Pass from Scotch Corner, being a Roman town (the medieval castle was built on the site of a Roman fort) guarding the pass. In the 18th and 19th centuries, before the coming of the railways, Brough was a major coaching town.

Warcop

The attractive village of Warcop is notable for the 12th century church of St Columba which was built on the site of a Roman camp. Each year an annual rush-bearing ceremony is held there. The fine 16th century bridge is the oldest surviving crossing of the River Eden.

Starting Point: Kirkby Stephen station. There are trains every two to three hours between Leeds, Settle and Carlisle and a summer Sunday service from Manchester, Preston and Blackburn.

Finishing/Return Point: Kirkby Stephen. Motorists should park in Kirkby Stephen town centre.

Distance: 38km (24 miles).

Time: 4¹/₂ hours.

Map: OS Landranger 91: Appleby.

Surfaces and Gradients: The route is all on tarmac lanes, although they are mostly narrow. There are several short but sometimes steep climbs totalling around 300m.

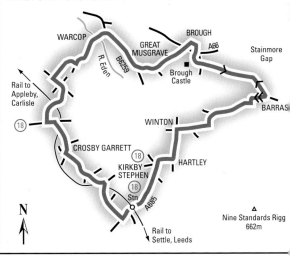

ROUTE 17
ACROSS THE STAINMORE GAP:
KIRKBY STEPHEN CIRCULAR

Traffic Conditions: Short sections along the very busy A685, with its heavy industrial traffic, must be negotiated with great care. Once away from this road, the ride is on quiet lanes with little traffic.

Facilities:
Cafés: Kirkby Stephen, Hartley, Brough Castle, Brough.
Pubs: Kirkby Stephen, Winton, Barras, Brough, Warcop.
Shops: Kirkby Stephen, Brough, Warcop.
WCs: Kirkby Stephen, Brough.
Tourist Information: Kirkby Stephen.
Youth Hostel: Kirkby Stephen.

ROUTE INSTRUCTIONS:
From Kirkby Stephen station cross the busy main road with care and turn right to follow the A685 down the hill into Kirkby Stephen. Go through the town centre, passing the traffic lights and the second mini-roundabout. Turn right on to the road signed for Hartley.

Turn left where the lane ends towards Winton. As you approach the village green turn right to follow the road to the hamlet of Rookby, then turn left to cross a stream and join another lane. Turn right and follow the lane as it dips by Duckintree and drops further by the River Belah before climbing steeply (1:5 or 20%) up the other side towards Barras.

Turn left just before Barras as the lane drops down (caution — hump-backed bridge and bend at the bottom of the hill!) and go straight ahead at the cross-roads. Continue to just before the lane meets the A685, where a track on the right takes you beneath the main road via an underpass. Turn

right to join a lane into Brough. Shortly afterwards Brough Castle is signposted on the left.

Follow the road down into Brough. Where the road becomes a dead end, take the path on the left and cross over the slip road to join the road going under the A66 bypass to the town centre.

From Brough take the next left to Great Musgrave, and then turn right on to the B6259. Follow this road as far as Warcop, turning left by the village green on to the road signed 'Bleatarn'. Leaving Warcop the road crosses the River Eden and climbs steadily. At Bleatarn the road bends sharply right; keep on this road and at the next junction go straight ahead. (If you wish to finish the ride in Appleby turn right here at the next junction.)

At the brow of the hill turn left then take the next right and follow this narrow lane until it emerges at a T-junction. Turn left then take the next right on to the road signed 'C Garrett'. The road descends into Crosby Garrett; keep on this lane as it follows the stream through the village. Turn left on to the road signed for Smardale, which turns out to be a very narrow lane.

The lane loses height before crossing a ford (a footbridge is also available) and climbing up the other side of the valley. Go past the cottages of Smardale; the road swings right over an old railway bridge. Follow the lane as it bends left under the railway and climbs again. Turn right at the next junction to cross the Settle–Carlisle railway line and continue on this road as it levels out past the sharp bend. The road drops down to the A685; turn left on to it and follow the road down to Kirkby Stephen station.

BETWEEN EDEN AND LUNE: KIRKBY STEPHEN TO APPLEBY

This is a ride to the upper Lune Valley beyond the northern Howgills, turning northwards down the little known Lyvennet Valley to return to the Eden Valley. A steady climb out of the Eden Valley is rewarded by extensive views across to the North Pennines. The spectacular limestone scenery in the early part of the ride is reminiscent of the Yorkshire Dales further south. Once past Great Asby Scar, the views to the south are of the dramatic Howgill Fells with the Shap Fells in the west. A visit to the village of Orton is followed by another climb over Crosby Ravensworth Fell into the Lyvennet Valley. Following the river northwards, the route runs through the slumbering villages of Crosby Ravensworth and the Meaburns before returning to the Eden and the old county town of Appleby.

BACKGROUND AND PLACES OF INTEREST:

Kirkby Stephen
For details see Route 17.

Orton
Lying in the upper Lune Valley and sheltered from the north by the massive forms of Crosby Ravensworth Fell and Great Asby Scar, the little village of Orton has a medieval church with a nave roof dating from the 15th century. George Whitehead, one of the founders of the Society of Friends (Quakers), was born here in 1636. Orton Scar, close to the village, is of particular interest and there are some notable limestone pavements in the area. Nearby Sunbiggin Tarn, passed on the ride, is a noted bird sanctuary, being a breeding area for black-headed gulls.

Crosby Ravensworth
This is another attractive village lying in the Lyvennet Valley. The church of St Lawrence dates back to Norman times and has two 12th century arches, a 14th century chapel, and two fonts — one from the 13th and one from the 17th century.

Kings Meaburn
This pretty stone village was once part of the manor of Meaburn. The Lord of the Manor, Hugh de Morville, one of King Henry II's knights, was implicated in the murder of Archbishop Thomas Becket in 1170. De Morville earned himself an evil reputation when it was alleged that he held back the crowd in Canterbury Cathedral whilst Thomas was murdered. Following Hugh's later rebellion against Henry in 1173, his lands were confiscated by the king who granted half to Hugh's sister, Maud, which became nearby Maulds Meaburn, whilst he retained the other half himself, which became known as Kings Meaburn.

Appleby
In a superb setting on a crook of the River Eden this lovely old town is dominated by its great Norman castle, the keep of which is remarkably similar to the Tower of London. Until 1974 Appleby was the county town of Westmorland. It is a market town and royal borough, the charters of which go back to 1174. There are many impressive Georgian and Victorian buildings, especially along its delightful main street, Boroughgate, which leads down past the market place to the impressive parish church in which the remarkable Lady Anne Clifford is buried. She was a great Cumbrian landowner and philanthropist who, in the late 17th century, built and endowed the lovely almshouses on the right as you descend Boroughgate. Also on the right is one of the oldest shops in the country, and there are fascinating courtyards as well as a lovely riverside area to explore with a good choice of pubs and cafés.

Above: The Howgills from the Lune Valley.

Above: Appleby station.

Starting Point: Kirkby Stephen station. Trains run approximately every two to three hours between Carlisle, Settle and Leeds. A summer Sunday service from Blackpool, Preston and Blackburn also operates. Motorists should park at Appleby (there is a car park at the station for rail users), take the train to Kirkby and cycle back to their car.

Finishing/Return Point: Appleby. Train service as above.

Distance: 49km (30¹/₂ miles).

Time: 4¹/₂ hours.

Map: OS Landranger 91: Appleby.

Surfaces and Gradients: The route takes place on tarmac surfaces throughout. These are generally moderately graded, but there are two major climbs with steep sections at Soulby (160m) and Orton (110m), and a small stiff climb out of Colby.

Traffic Conditions: Traffic generally is light, apart from along the A685 between Kirkby Stephen station and the town where great care is required.

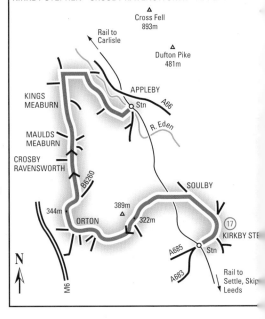

ROUTE 18
BETWEEN EDEN AND LUNE
KIRKBY STEPHEN - CROSBY RAVENSWORTH - APPLEBY

Facilities:
Cafés: Kirkby Stephen, Orton, Appleby.
Pubs: Kirkby Stephen, Orton, Bolton, Appleby.
Shops: Kirkby Stephen, Orton, Bolton, Appleby.
WCs: Kirkby Stephen, Orton, Appleby.
Tourist Information: Kirkby Stephen, Appleby.
Youth Hostels: Kirkby Stephen, Dufton near
Appleby (6km [3³/₄ miles]).

ROUTE INSTRUCTIONS:

From Kirkby Stephen station turn right outside
the station drive/access path and cross carefully
on to the very busy A685, following the main
road downhill as it curves into the town centre.
Take care as this is a dangerous and unpleasant
stretch of road, but with a fairly quick descent it is
soon over.

From Kirkby Stephen town centre turn left at
Silver Street and follow the road signed for Soulby.
In Soulby take the first left over the bridge and
then the road signed for Orton. The road ascends
steadily, climbing over the railway and dropping
into a small valley before resuming the ascent.

At Whygill Head turn left on the
Orton road over a cattle grid before
making the final ascent of the summit
from where there are excellent views.
Following the Orton road, the route
begins its descent, passing Sunbiggin
Tarn. Continue straight ahead towards
the hamlet of Raisbeck, where you turn
right and continue as far as Orton.

At the T-junction turn right on to the
Appleby road and go through the
village centre. Follow the B6260 up the
steep hill out of the village. At the
summit turn left for Crosby
Ravensworth. This road soon drops

Below: Orton village.

Right: A quiet lane near Appleby.

steadily into the Lyvennet Valley and Crosby
Ravensworth. Continue through Crosby
Ravensworth to Maulds Meaburn, following the
road as it keeps on the left bank of the river,
passing the large village green. Just outside
Maulds Meaburn turn right to go over the bridge
towards Kings Meaburn. At the next junction turn
left to go up into Kings Meaburn.

Follow the road through Kings Meaburn; after
the village a gradual descent leads down to a T-
junction. Turn right on to the Appleby road. At
Bolton turn right at the crossroads taking the road
signed for Colby. Follow this through to Appleby.
At the junction turn left and take the right fork
round past the castle entrance into Boroughgate,
the wide main street and market place; the church
with its ornate Buttermarket gateway is a notable
feature at the bottom of the town.

From the main street follow the road right, over
the bridge across the River Eden and turn left.
Follow this road for a few metres before turning
sharp right up the steep hill to Appleby's attractive
and welcoming railway station (signed).

ON THE EDGE OF ENNERDALE: BRAYSTONES TO WHITEHAVEN

The ride leads from the exposed Cumbrian coastline at Braystones, a small halt on the West Cumbria line between Sellafield and St Bees Head. Running above the riverside, the route follows quiet lanes through Egremont into the fellscape of Ennerdale, in the western part of the Lake District mountains. Climbing out of the valley the rider can choose to extend the route to go further into Ennerdale (and perhaps stay at Black Sail Hut youth hostel) or to return to Whitehaven. Using the well-constructed C2C cycleway, a long gentle descent out of the fells to Whitehaven ensures a pleasant latter stage of the ride, with easy navigation.

BACKGROUND AND PLACES OF INTEREST:

Egremont
Set in well-maintained grounds, the ruins of Egremont Castle make an impressive feature above the little town. The castle is an excellent example of the motte and bailey construction favoured by the Normans. It was established in 1120 by William de Meschines who had been given the Barony of Egremont. The castle was attacked by Robert the Bruce's forces in 1315, which led to its major renovation and expansion, including the construction of the Great Hall. Although much destroyed by the ravages of time, one of its imposing walls still dominates the site. The site also has a cross dating from 1200 which had been moved from the town market. The old town centre has a market place, narrow streets and old houses, one dating from Tudor times.

Ennerdale Bridge
The village forms the entrance to Ennerdale. The churchyard was the setting for Wordsworth's poem The Two Brothers. The dale, originally known as 'Einarr's Dale' is one of the few larger Lakeland valleys still inaccessible by car. It is worth going to the end of the tarmac lane beyond Croasdale just to enjoy the superb views of Ennerdale Water, one of the quietest of the major lakes, with its great backcloth of open fells. A bridlepath leads alongside Ennerdale Water into the high Lakeland fells, going as far as Black Sail Hut youth hostel which is also inaccessible by car. Footpaths from the upper valley lead to the peaks of Great Gable and Hay Stacks.

C2C Route Rowrah–Whitehaven
This section of what is one of Britain's most popular cycle routes follows the course of an old mineral railway. Along the route many imaginative metallic sculptures point to the railway's former function and the region's industrial past.

Below: The Beacon Museum, Whitehaven.

Whitehaven

Whitehaven is one of Cumbria's, and England's, most famous ports. It grew rapidly from a village of just nine cottages in 1693 to a town of over 2,000 by the end of the 17th century, its growth stimulated by the export of coal from nearby mines owned by the Lowther family. But it was in the 18th century that the port really grew in size and importance, at one time being larger than Liverpool, and in 1788 it was the victim of a pirate raid by the so-called founder of the American Navy, John Paul Jones.

Whitehaven has an attractive, mainly Georgian, harbour which is now home to a new museum, 'The Beacon', which describes the history of Whitehaven. The town has many shops and services and is an ideal place to stay overnight.

Below: Riding along the C2C Route near Whitehaven.

Starting Point: Braystones Halt. Six trains each way per day call at this little station on the Barrow–Carlisle line. These include useful mid-morning and early afternoon trains in both directions to Braystones. This station is a request stop, so ask the guard, at the latest by the previous station, for the train to stop. There is no Sunday service, however. Motorists should park in Whitehaven, take the outward train and cycle back to their car.

Finishing/Return Point: Whitehaven. There are trains to Barrow (and Lancaster) and more frequently to Carlisle.

Distance: 32km (20 miles).

Time: 3¹/₂ hours.

Map: OS Landranger 89: West Cumbria.

Surfaces and Gradients: The route follows tarmac roads throughout, with short climbs before and after Egremont and a steeper climb between Ennerdale Bridge and Kirkland or Croasdale.

Traffic Conditions: The roads and lanes are quiet throughout, but there are busy roads as you enter Whitehaven.

Below: Egremont Castle.

Facilities:
Cafés: Egremont, Whitehaven.
Pubs: Egremont, Whitehaven,
Ennerdale Bridge.
Shops: Egremont, Whitehaven.
WCs: Egremont, Whitehaven.
Tourist Information: Whitehaven,
Egremont.
Youth Hostels: Ennerdale,
Black Sail Hut.

ROUTE 19
ON THE EDGE OF ENNERDALE
BRAYSTONES - EGREMONT - WHITEHAVEN

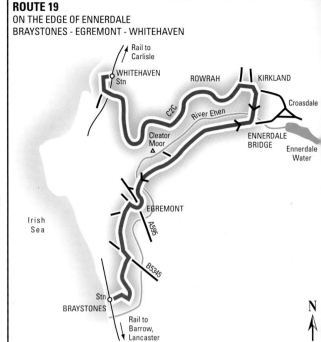

ROUTE INSTRUCTIONS:

From Braystones Halt exit by the track which is marked by the gate at the end of the platform. Follow the track as it climbs away from the coastline and meets a tarmac lane shortly afterwards. Turn right and take the next left a few metres further, on the road signed for Egremont.

Follow this lane as far as the T-junction then turn left (Egremont is signed right). A short distance further on turn right on this lane which is also signed for Egremont. Follow this lane through to Egremont, turning right at the junction with the larger road for Egremont town centre.

Where the road ends in Egremont town centre, take the next left, Church Road. Turn right, taking the underpass beneath the bypass road. Turn left and follow this street up to the junction by a petrol station. Turn right, following this back road out of Egremont, which is signed for Ennerdale Bridge a short distance further. Dropping down to the river, the road climbs on the other side of the valley.

This lane climbs steadily and drops again to the riverside; turn right at the junction and continue to Ennerdale Bridge. Follow the road to the bottom of Ennerdale Bridge.

For Ennerdale turn right on the Croasdale road and follow this road through Croasdale to Ennerdale Water. The road becomes a track here and beyond are the upper reaches of Ennerdale and the isolated Black Sail Hut, a youth hostel in a dramatic mountain setting. If returning from upper Ennerdale, go back via Croasdale and Kirkland.

To continue to Whitehaven follow the same road for Kirkland, but take special care here as traffic speeds along this narrow lane. The climb out can be a little unpleasant, but it is a relatively short section.

At Kirkland the hilltop is reached; turn left to join the C2C cycle route. Follow the blue C2C signs as they direct you down left by the school and right on to a path through a gap in a hedge.

The path winds down to Rowrah where it widens to a track and then a tarmac cyclepath. Follow the blue cast-iron signs for Whitehaven as you begin an easy gradual descent out of the fells.

The C2C route winds through the outer estates of Whitehaven before emerging at a main road. Follow the road into Whitehaven town centre with the harbour appearing on the left.

For the railway station keep in the left lane and follow the road through the town centre traffic lights. The station is hidden behind a supermarket car park and petrol station. It is down the second left turn in the supermarket zone, with only small signs to betray its existence.

Above: Whitehaven harbour.

CARTMEL AND HUMPHREY HEAD: GRANGE-OVER-SANDS TO CARK

This ride from Grange-over-Sands through the gentle coastal countryside of Furness, on the southern edge of the Lake District National Park, is not to be hurried. Allow time to explore the delightful village of Cartmel with its great priory church, and perhaps to leave the bike in order to stroll to the summit of Humphrey Head with its spectacular views of Morecambe Bay, before catching the train back to Grange and beyond.

BACKGROUND AND PLACES OF INTEREST:

Grange-over-Sands

Grange-over-Sands is a quiet, even sleepy resort, which, despite its name, doesn't have a beach, the sands being the extensive mud flats and quicksand of Morecambe Bay which are crossed, near Kents Bank station, by an ancient right of way once regularly used (incredible as it now seems) by horse-drawn coaches. Regular walks across the sands at low tide are organised by the Morecambe Bay Queen's Guide. Grange itself has delightful gardens, a long promenade, an attractive main street with pleasant Edwardian architecture and a choice of cafés, shops and pubs, as well as one of the prettiest railway stations in Cumbria, complete with its own bookshop.

Lindale

Lindale, with its steep main street, is not really a tourist village, but there are winding, narrow streets, an old church and pub, and fine views across Morecambe Bay. The village also has the Wilkinson Monument, erected in memory of Cumbria ironmaster John Wilkinson who helped build the world's first cast-iron bridge at Ironbridge, Shropshire, and the world's first iron boats. He lived at nearby Castle Head, now a field studies centre, where he is buried.

Cartmel and Cartmel Priory

One of the prettiest villages in Cumbria, Cartmel has an attractive cluster of cottages, shops and old inns set around an intimate square complete with ancient market cross. The village is dominated by its huge priory church. The Priory was founded by Augustinian Canons in 1188; its massive 14th century gatehouse and the Church of St Mary and Michael with its splendid east window survive. In the graveyard are several memorials to travellers who drowned on the quicksands attempting to cross Morecambe Bay. At the cross-roads towards Allithwaite look for the carved panel set in the wall informing coach travellers that Lancaster is just 15 miles away across the sands — if you don't drown en route.

Below: Grange-over-Sands — the public park and the lake.

Humphrey Head

This magnificent promontory of limestone jutting out into Morecambe Bay is now a 23-hectare nature reserve managed by the Cumbria Wildlife Trust. The only real sea cliff in this part of Cumbria, the headland rises to 53m to form a splendid viewpoint. According to local legend, when, in 1281, King Edward I decreed that every wolf in England be exterminated, the last lone wolf survived at Humphrey Head. It is now a haven for much wildlife, including orange lichens, hoary rockrose, maidenhair fern, belladonna and juniper. There is access to the headland on a footpath by the entrance of the outdoor centre (you cannot cycle on the footpath so park your machines carefully). The public road gives access to a small car park and the cliffs where, at low tide, Humphrey Head Point can be accessed — but take care as the tides come in quickly, the sands are treacherous and the cliffs are unstable and dangerous.

Flookborough

Once a market town (its market place survives), Flookborough was given its charter in 1278. It has long been a fishing village, still celebrated for the catching of local Morecambe Bay shrimps.

Cark-in-Cartmel

This pleasant village is less than a kilometre from Holker Hall, a magnificent country house with parkland which is open to visitors during the summer months. Amongst the sumptuous interiors and furnishings in the house, there is an embroidered panel said to have been worked by Mary, Queen of Scots. The hall also contains the Lakeland Motor Museum with over 100 veteran and vintage cars, motor cycles and bikes.

Starting Point: Grange-over-Sands station on the railway line between Lancaster and Barrow. There are frequent trains from Manchester, Bolton, Preston, Lancaster and Barrow, and plenty of car parking in the town centre.

Finishing/Return Point: Cark & Cartmel station, on the same line. A return can be made to Grange via the main road from Allithwaite (an extra two miles) for those wanting a circular ride, which avoids catching the train back from Cark, but the B5277 is a busy and fairly urbanised road and the short train ride is much nicer. (This ride can also be combined with Route 21 from Cark to Windermere.)

Distance: 22km (14 miles).

Above: Cartmel Priory.

Time: 3 hours.

Maps: OS Landranger 96: Barrow-in-Furness & South Lakeland; 97: Kendal & Morecambe.

Surfaces and Gradients: The ride is on good surfaces throughout, though some gravelly stretches on the descents near Broughton Lodge and Allithwaite require care. Gradients are generally moderate, the big exception being the very steep climb through Lindale, especially on the narrow lane west of Lindale towards Hampsfield where walking is recommended for all but the strongest cyclists.

Traffic Conditions: The first 600m along the B5277 out of Grange are fairly busy and also between the Meathop lane end and Lindale. Otherwise, the lanes are quiet throughout with some virtually traffic-free stretches.

Facilities:
Cafés: Grange-over-Sands, Cartmel.
Pubs: Grange-over-Sands, Lindale, Cartmel, Flookborough, Cark.
Shops: Grange-over-Sands, Lindale, Cartmel, Flookborough, Cark.
WCs: Grange-over-Sands (at the station and in the park), Cartmel, Flookborough, Cark.
Tourist Information: Grange-over-Sands.

ROUTE INSTRUCTIONS:

From Grange station turn right outside the car park on to the busy B5277, and follow the road for about 600m to where there is a junction with an unmarked lane to the right. This leads along a quiet lane, parallel to the railway, which eventually goes northwards and ascends a low hill to the hamlet of Meathop. Turn left at the junction below Meathop and continue to where the lane turns sharp right before joining the old main road to Barrow just south of the traffic island on the A590.

Turn left along the road, now the B5277 again, which still has more than enough fast-moving traffic to require some care. Keep ahead for 2km (1¼ miles) until you reach the village of Lindale, going straight ahead at the traffic island and up the steep main street. About half-way along the street, past a waterfall, take the lane on the left, which curves through the centre of the pretty village past the church and school. Turn right at the end and right again to join the B5271 past the junction with Lindale's main street. Go left here, continuing uphill, but almost at the brow of the hill turn sharp left up another narrow, unmarked lane which climbs extremely steeply (walking advised) over the back of Hampsfell. Avoid the turning to Hampsfield and cross the brow of the hill from where there are superb views of the Lakeland peaks and ridges straight ahead. The road now drops steeply into the Vale of Cartmel; keep left at each of the next two junctions signed to Cartmel, past Broughton Lodge to Cartmel. As you come into the village, take the first narrow lane which passes the priory church to enter the village square under the arch of the priory gateway.

Return along the road past the King's Head Inn which passes the right side of the church, keeping right at the next junction towards Allithwaite. Follow the Grange and Allithwaite signs at the next junction (note the carved inscription on the wall indicating the coach route to Lancaster), but where this road climbs and swings to the left at a junction, take the minor lane marked to Templand straight ahead. This lane soon reaches the western edge of Allithwaite at Templand Bank. Where it descends to a three-way junction by a large oak tree and seat, take the middle lane half to the right — Locker Lane. This descends very steeply (care required) to reach the B5277. Cross directly ahead; the lane is now signed 'Humphrey Head 1½ miles'. Follow this, turning right at the first junction to pass Wraysholme Hall with its impressive fortified pele tower, then go over the level crossing. Turn left

at the T-junction, the lane now curving southwards before heading to Humphrey Head. Follow the lane to the right, past the entrance to the outdoor centre, to where it terminates at the small car park on the foreshore.

Return by the same route to the T-Junction south of the level crossing. For Grange-over-Sands return the same way to the B5277 past Wraysholme Hall and then follow this main road direct to Grange. For Cark keep straight ahead on the lane past Winder Moor and Cark airfield, turning right at the junction to Flookborough where you keep straight ahead past the market place along Station Road. If you are catching a train back to Grange, Carnforth or Lancaster, or returning from Cark village centre, do not go into the station by the main entrance, but continue a further 100m over the railway bridge, turning first right along the (unmarked) and potholed station drive — this saves carrying your bike over the narrow footbridge.

Above: Cartmel village and the Priory.

ROUTE 20
CARTMEL AND HUMPHREY HEAD

FIELD BROUGHTON
LINDALE
A590
MEATHOP
CARTMEL
Rail to Carnforth, Lancaster
Rail to Barrow
B5278
B5271
Stn
GRANGE-OVER-SANDS
ALLITHWAITE
CARK
Stn
Kents Bank Stn
FLOOKBURGH
HUMPHREY HEAD

N

🚲 ROUTE 21

BY FURNESS FELLS TO WINDERMERE: CARK TO WINDERMERE

A ride through the varied landscape of the Furness Fells into the southern Lake District, from the gentle landscape of low-lying fields near Cartmel through to the wild-looking, wooded foothills of the Furness Fells. A drop into the Leven Valley takes the rider through the thick oak woods on the western side of Windermere, passing the hamlet of Finsthwaite, the museum of Stott Park Bobbin Mill and close to the Lakeside Wildlife Exhibition Centre, then alongside England's largest lake, Windermere. Winding through the trees with occasional views across the lake, the ride then drops down to the ferry for the crossing over to Bowness for the final leg up to Windermere station.

BACKGROUND AND PLACES OF INTEREST:

Cartmel Village and Priory
See Route 20.

Haverthwaite
Haverthwaite is the starting point of the Lakeside & Haverthwaite Railway. This popular 6km (3¾ mile) steam railway (trains run on most days between April and November) links at Lakeside with the Windermere boat service. The branch line was originally built by the Furness Railway Co and opened in 1868 to carry Victorian trippers from its main line at Ulverston to link with the company's steam launches to Bowness and Ambleside. After the line closed in the 1960s and was taken over by preservationists, the construction of the Haverthwaite bypass (A590) on the old trackbed prevented the railway from continuing southwards, though trains and boats for Bowness and Ambleside still connect at the little resort of Lakeside.

Above: A view across the Vale of Cartmel.

Stott Park Bobbin Mill

This little museum set in the woodlands at Finsthwaite is based on a unique mill which was built in 1835 to supply wooden bobbins and cotton reels made from local wood to the mills of the Lancashire textile industry, a use which continued until 1971. The museum continues to make bobbins, and guides explain the process. On some days you can see in operation a static steam engine that was used to drive the machinery.

Windermere

Strictly speaking, the name 'Windermere' refers to the lake and not the town, which only received that name when its railway station was built in the 1840s. Windermere is England's largest lake, being 17km (10^1/$_2$ miles) long, 1.6km (1 mile) wide at its widest point and 64m deep at its deepest point. As well as being a major tourist attraction for boating, rowing, fishing and a variety of water sports, it is also rich in aquatic wildlife, including the unique char, a large fish which inhabits the lake and which may have been trapped in Windermere since Ice Age times. The Lakeside Aquatics Centre (follow the signs just after Finsthwaite to get there) has an exhibition centre on local wildlife with an underwater display section actually beneath the lake.

Bowness-on-Windermere

Bowness and Windermere are twin popular resort towns along the eastern side of Lake Windermere with a multitude of shops, cafés and guest houses. Bowness, with its ancient church, old inns and narrow main street, is far older than Windermere, the upper town which grew in the later 19th and early 20th century as suburban development around the rail station. There is a Lake District National Park centre and tourist information centre in Bowness close to the main promenade, with exhibitions, displays and a wide range of literature.

Below: Sailing on Windermere.
Cumbria Tourist Board

Below right: Bowness Bay Pier.
Cumbria Tourist Board

Windermere is also a key transport interchange for the southern Lake District, with a busy branch railway to and from Oxenholme on the main line and buses reaching most parts of the Lake District. There is a cycle hire centre at the station.

Starting Point: Cark & Cartmel station. There are approximately hourly trains to Carnforth and Lancaster, with many continuing to Preston, Bolton, Manchester Oxford Road and Piccadilly. Motorists should park in Lancaster, take the outward train to Cark and return from Windermere.

Finishing/Return Point: Windermere. The station has approximately hourly trains to Oxenholme and Lancaster, with many continuing to Preston, Bolton, Manchester Oxford Road and Piccadilly. (Alternatively, you can join Route 22 to finish in Ulverston.)

Distance: 29km (18 miles).

Time: 3^1/$_2$ hours.

Maps: OS Landranger 97: Kendal & Morecambe.

Surfaces and Gradients: The ride is on tarmac throughout, with one significant climb between Cartmel and Backbarrow.

Traffic Conditions: The ride takes place on reasonably quiet lanes as far as Bowness, apart from having to cross the A590, but traffic can always be busy in the Lake District, especially between Bowness and Windermere during the holiday period, and even out of the main season.

Facilities:
Cafés: Cartmel, Lakeside, Bowness, Windermere.
Pubs: Cark, Cartmel, Bowness, Windermere.
Shops: Cartmel, Bowness, Windermere.
WCs: Cark, Cartmel, Bowness, Windermere.
Tourist Information: Bowness, Windermere.
Youth Hostel: Windermere.
Cycle Hire: Windermere station.

ROUTE INSTRUCTIONS:

From Cark & Cartmel station exit by the car park on the Barrow-bound platform, or along the rear drive if coming from Barrow. Turn right on to the road and follow it over the railway and into the village of Cark. Turn right up the slope for Cartmel and follow the lane for the next 4km (2 miles) to Cartmel. Take the second left, passing Cartmel Priory and entering the central court by an ancient archway. Turn right and take the right fork to leave Cartmel by the racecourse.

Follow the road signed for Haverthwaite. There is a steady ascent through the scrubby hills above. Ignore the left turn-off as the road flattens out and passes a country club before the final summit. A steep drop follows. Turn right part-way down to continue down the hill to Backbarrow.

With great care turn right on to the A590 before taking an immediate left turn. If the traffic is too busy, use the traffic island just ahead. The lane descends through Lakeside holiday village; turn right just over the bridge. The lane then runs under the railway bridge and ascends; keep on this lane as it runs deep through the woods. At the next junction go straight ahead on the road signed for Finsthwaite and through the long hamlet. Where the road descends to a wider road, turn left and continue as far as the (back) gates of Graythwaite Hall.

Turn right to head down to Cunsey and Windermere ferry. Continue along the lane and turn right to drop down to the ferry stage by the lake. The car, foot and cycle ferry operates every few minutes. Once across the ferry, keep ahead into Bowness, turning right along the busy foreshore and up the crowded main street to Windermere station, which is on the right before you reach the T-junction with the A591.

(If you wish to combine this ride with Route 22, ignore the turn-off for the ferry and climb up the slope to Far Sawrey.)

Above: Boats moored in Bowness Bay.
Cumbria Tourist Board

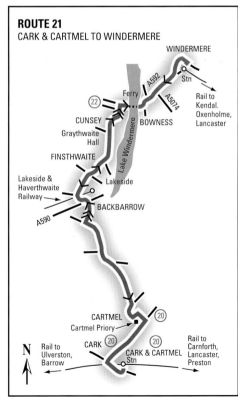

ROUTE 21
CARK & CARTMEL TO WINDERMERE

Below: Old Man of Coniston.

ALONG THE SHORES OF CONISTON WATER: WINDERMERE TO ULVERSTON

This route through the Furness Fells of southern Lakeland runs from the town and lake of Windermere up and around Esthwaite Water to the popular village of Hawkshead, before climbing Hawkshead Hill and crossing over to the shores of Coniston Water. Exploring the quiet and wooded east side of Coniston Water, the route follows the gently contoured lane southwards before ascending steadily over Lowick Common to take a back road into Ulverston, culminating in a steady descent into the town.

BACKGROUND AND PLACES OF INTEREST:

Windermere
See Route 21.

Esthwaite Water
Esthwaite Water is one of the smallest but prettiest of the southern lakes. Little more than a tarn, with reed-fringed banks and fine views it remains totally unspoiled.

Hawkshead
This extremely pretty village is where Wordsworth attended his local grammar school and described his childhood experiences in The Prelude, and is close to where (at Near Sawrey) authoress Beatrix Potter achieved worldwide fame with her illustrated 'Peter Rabbit' books. The village has inevitably suffered a tide of tourism, as large car parks, and outdoor equipment and clothing stores on the outskirts confirm, but it retains much of its attractiveness, and has a wide choice of facilities.

Brantwood
Brantwood was the home of artist, essayist and philosopher John Ruskin for the last years of his life from 1872 until 1900. The house and gardens with their magnificent views across Coniston Water to Coniston Old Man are open to the public, and bookshop and restaurant facilities are available.

Coniston Water
This particularly beautiful lake was in 1967 the scene of tragedy when Donald Campbell's ill-fated attempt at the world water speed record of over 300mph ended in disaster when his boat *Bluebird* went out of control. A more tranquil form of

transport is provided by the lake launches, which provide a useful ferry service, including the remarkable steam launch *Gondola*, built in 1859 for the Furness Railway, abandoned for many years at the bottom of the lake, and now restored and operated as a public cruise boat by the National Trust. It is regularly to be seen gently and silently steaming across the lake's still waters.

Ulverston

The busy little market town of Ulverston, with its handsome station built by the Furness Railway, blends a certain amount of industry with tourism. The town is overlooked by what appears to be a tall lighthouse — the Hoad Monument — which is a memorial to Sir John Barrow, a founder member of the Royal Geographical Society. It also has Britain's shortest canal for sea-going craft, which links the town with a deep channel across Morecambe Bay. Ulverston is also the birthplace of Stan Laurel of Laurel and Hardy film comedy fame, and there is a Laurel and Hardy Museum in the town. The town also has a heritage centre, whilst Swarthmoor Hall, just to the south of Ulverston, was the home of Margaret Fell, one of the 17th century pioneers of the worldwide Quaker movement.

Starting Point: Windermere. There are approximately hourly trains from Oxenholme, Lancaster and Preston, with through trains from Manchester Piccadilly and Manchester Airport.

Finishing/Return Point: Ulverston station. There are approximately hourly trains to Carnforth and Lancaster, with many trains continuing to Preston, Bolton and Manchester.

Distance: 37km (23 miles).

Time: 4 hours.

Maps: OS Landranger 97: Kendal & Morecambe; 96: Barrow in Furness & South Lakeland.

Surfaces and Gradients: The ride takes place on good tarmac lanes and roads throughout. There are three moderate climbs of around 100m.

Traffic Conditions: Traffic should be generally moderate.

Below: Coniston Water seen through trees on a back lane.

Facilities:
Cafés: Windermere, Bowness, Hawkshead, Brantwood, Ulverston.
Pubs: Windermere, Bowness, Far Sawrey, Near Sawrey, Hawkshead, Lowick Bridge, Ulverston.
Shops: Windermere, Bowness, Hawkshead, Ulverston.
WCs: Windermere, Bowness, Hawkshead, Ulverston.
Tourist Information: Windermere, Bowness, Ulverston.
Youth Hostels: Windermere, Hawkshead, Coniston.

ROUTE INSTRUCTIONS:

From Windermere railway station turn left past Booth's supermarket to the junction and then left down the busy main street to Bowness. Keep left along the lake promenade area, turning right for the ferry which runs every few minutes. Let the cars leave first after the ferry arrives at the far shore to enjoy a quieter ride.

From the ferry stage, follow the Coniston road up the hill and through Far Sawrey, turning left at Near Sawrey down the road signed for Lakeside.

Follow this lane downhill, keeping straight ahead at the next turn-off to reach the far end of the lake, crossing over the river draining Esthwaite Water. The lane bends round the edge of the lake before joining a wider road; turn right on to this road and continue as far as Hawkshead.

At the village turn left along the road marked for buses only, to get to the centre. Continue straight ahead and cut through the short pedestrian precinct by the Queens Head Hotel to rejoin the road.

Turn left on to the main road and then take the next left signed for Coniston. This lane makes a steady ascent and keep on this past the summit. The descent through the woods is steep; turn left part-way down, taking the lane signed for the east side of lake.

The lane descends steadily and then more gradually to the lakeside, passing Brantwood. After 10km (6 miles) of beautiful, quiet riding with constant views of the lake through the trees, the road ends at a T-junction at Lowick Bridge. Turn right here to cross the river, and then cross straight over the A5084. Ignoring the fork

left, follow the lane as it ascends gradually to the A5092. Cross straight ahead to the lane opposite (signed Ulverston). It ascends gradually; ignore the turn-off and continue along this lane until it meets the B5281.

Turn left on to the B5281 and follow this road as it begins the long descent into Ulverston. When the road ends at a roundabout, take the third turning to go through the town centre. Go straight ahead at the traffic lights over the A590 dual carriageway to continue to the station. Ulverston railway station is 150m further on the right; the entrance is down a short slope.

Right:
Wordsworth Street, Hawkshead.

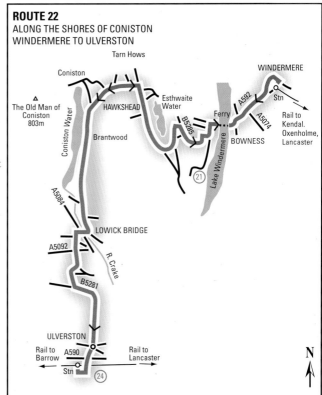

ROUTE 22
ALONG THE SHORES OF CONISTON
WINDERMERE TO ULVERSTON

Tarn Hows

Coniston

WINDERMERE

The Old Man of Coniston 803m

Coniston Water

HAWKSHEAD

Esthwaite Water

A592

Stn

Rail to Kendal, Oxenholme, Lancaster

B5285

Ferry

A5074

Brantwood

BOWNESS

Lake Windermere

21

A5084

LOWICK BRIDGE

A5092

R. Crake

B5281

ULVERSTON

Rail to Barrow

A590

Rail to Lancaster

Stn

24

N

🚲 ROUTE 23

ULLSWATER: PENRITH CIRCULAR

This is a ride to enjoy the splendours of Ullswater, one of the most dramatically beautiful of the English lakes. Using the old town of Penrith as a gateway, the route follows the little River Eamont to Ullswater, going along the lake shore with some spectacular views across the lake into the high Lakeland fells. Climbing away from the lake by Aira Force, the route crosses a low pass to Matterdale End, with views north and east to the Scottish mountains and the North Pennines, before continuing to the village of Greystoke and finishing with an easy descent back to Penrith.

BACKGROUND AND PLACES OF INTEREST:

Penrith

This market town is full of character and interest, with a ruined castle (opposite the railway station) which once belonged to Richard III, a covered market cross in the Cornmarket, a town hall based on two houses designed by Robert Adam, an unusually fine Georgian parish church, a small museum in the town's 17th century Robinson's School, several venerable inns, and a choice of shops, cafés and pubs. Penrith Beacon, a prominent landmark on the hill immediately above the town with its stone 'pike' built in 1719, was used in 1745 to warn the townspeople of the coming of Bonnie Prince Charlie's Jacobite army which marched through Penrith on its way south to eventual defeat by the Duke of Cumberland's forces.

Dalemain House

This 18th century mansion, built around an earlier Elizabethan House, stands in magnificent parkland and is open to the public during the summer months. It has collections of antique furniture and paintings, the Westmorland & Cumberland Yeomanry Museum, a 16th century great barn with old agricultural implements and the Fell Pony Museum.

Pooley Bridge

As well as its pubs and cafés, the tourist village of Pooley Bridge is noted for its unusual Norman church with a rare central tower. In the summer months steamers leave the landing stage at regular intervals for Howtown and Glenridding.

Ullswater

Ullswater, in its steep and narrow valley overlooked by Helvellyn and a circle of spectacular fells, is one of the most dramatically beautiful of all the lakes. It is also one of the longest and deepest, being 14.5km (9 miles) in length and over 65m deep in places. Because of its location on the northeastern edge of the Lake District National Park, it is rather less heavily visited than its more central neighbours, though there is a popular ferry service along the lake between Pooley Bridge and Glenridding.

Aira Force

This romantically beautiful waterfall is formed by the little Aira Beck as it plunges down a narrow and rocky ravine known as Aira Glen. Now owned and managed by the National Trust, the Force is a popular visitor attraction, accessed by footpath from the NT car park (small fee payable).

Below: The gardens at Dalemain House. *Cumbria Tourist Board*

Greystoke

This charming village, with its grey stone cottages and village green, no longer suffers constant industrial traffic which now uses the nearby A66 to Workington. It has a fine church, mostly dating from the 15th century, with some carved misericords and a beautiful east window. Outside the church is a sanctuary stone marking the point at which anyone fleeing to the church was safe from persecution. Greystoke Castle, the ornate, castellated mansion close to the village, dates back to a pele tower built in 1353, although it was largely restored in the 19th century.

Below: The Lady of the Lake on Ullswater.
Cumbria Tourist Board

Bottom: Ullswater.

Starting Point: Penrith station. There are approximately hourly trains from Lancaster, Preston and Carlisle. Some trains also run direct from Manchester Piccadilly. (Booking for cycles is advised for these services.) There is adequate car parking in Penrith town centre.

Finishing/Return Point: Penrith station.

Alternative Start/Finish Point: Langwathby station, on the Settle–Carlisle line with direct services from Carlisle, Settle and Leeds etc, also makes a good link with other rides in the Eden Valley (Routes 16, 17, 18, 27 and 28). Langwathby is 9km (5^1/$_2$ miles) from Penrith on the A686 (Alston) road.

Distance: 40km (25 miles); Langwathby option: 58km (36 miles).

Time: 4 hours

Map: OS Landranger 90: Penrith & Keswick

Surfaces and Gradients: The ride is on tarmac surfaces throughout. It is hilly from Penrith to and along Ullswater, with one steep climb from Ullswater to Matterdale End (160m), then downhill or easy gradients from Matterdale End to Greystoke and Penrith.

Traffic Conditions: Traffic should be generally moderate, although roads to and alongside Ullswater are much busier with tourist traffic during the main holiday season. Care is required when crossing the main A66 trunk road.

Facilities:
Cafés: Penrith, Pooley Bridge, Aira Force.
Pubs: Penrith, Stainton, Pooley Bridge, Watermillock, Dockray, Greystoke.
Shops: Penrith, Greystoke.
WCs: Penrith, Pooley Bridge, Aira Force (Ullswater).
Tourist Information: Penrith.
Youth Hostels: Helvellyn (Glenridding), Patterdale.

ROUTE INSTRUCTIONS:
From Penrith station turn left at the entrance and at the roundabout turn left again along the B5288 signed for Greystoke.

(If starting the ride from Langwathby station you should join the A686 from the station and turn left. Follow it as far as Carleton traffic lights then turn right in to Winters Park and follow this road into Penrith. Turn right at the end of the road and go through the town centre's one-way system; where the station is signed, bend right at Castlegate. To start the route turn right at the roundabout, and at the next roundabout take the B5288 Greystoke road.)

Follow the B5288 over the railway line and then, leaving town, go over the M6 motorway. Take the second lane on the left, signed Stainton, just past the stone obelisk of Greystoke Pillar.

This lane goes up a slope. At the next junction turn left to descend shortly under the A66 and into the village of Stainton. Go straight ahead at the crossroads, keeping ahead through the village centre. At the T-junction beyond the village turn left, following the lane down to the A592. Turn right on to the A592 which follows the River Eamont, passing the entrance to Dalemain House and parkland before rounding a hill and descending gently to the shore of Ullswater. For Pooley Bridge village with its cafés and pub, turn left at the junction.

Otherwise, continue along the A592 as far as Aira Force. If you choose to visit the

Force, park your cycle in the car park. The route continues on the A5091 by turning right just after the car park. This road (although an A-road, it is nearer to a minor road in character) climbs steadily, passing the hamlet of Dockray. Turn right at Matterdale End; the lane is signed as the C2C route to Penrith. This road soon reaches its summit; keep on this road, ignoring the C2C turn-off soon after the descent. At the junction with the very busy A66 trunk road, cross straight ahead (taking great care with the fast-moving traffic), on to the B5288. Take the next turn right and then left following the B5288 and signs for Greystoke. The road then begins a long gentle descent into Greystoke village.

Keep on the same road through the village (unless you wish to take the signed National Cycle Route 71 route to Penrith, which is 5km [3 miles] longer, but a little quieter). If continuing on the perfectly acceptable B5288, the road gains height on leaving Greystoke, before a gradual descent direct to Penrith.

At the roundabout, turn right heading towards the station, and at the next roundabout turn right again, afterwards taking the second turning on the right to the station.

(If heading for Langwathby — a further 9km [5¹⁄₂ miles] — turn left at the first roundabout to go to the town centre. Continue through the town centre, turning right down Middlegate and then left at Roper Street for Carleton. Continue along this road out of Penrith to join the A686 at Carleton. Turn left for Langwathby, the station being on the right after passing the village green.)

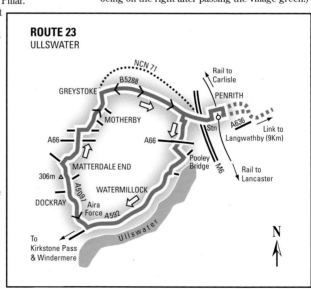

ROUTE 23
ULLSWATER

FURNESS ABBEY AND ROA ISLAND: DALTON IN FURNESS TO ULVERSTON

The ride starts from the busy town of Dalton, then soon passes through undulating terrain to the impressive ruins of Furness Abbey. Following a valley, the route skirts the edge of the industrial town of Barrow before heading out to the fascinating Roa Island, connected to the mainland by only a thin strip of land. The route then returns to the mainland to continue along the lovely coast road of Furness with wide panoramic views across Morecambe Bay. Heading inland, the route passes Gleaston, and Little and Great Urswick before ascending through pastoral countryside to the outskirts of Ulverston.

Below: Roa Island.

Inset: Crossroads near Gleaston.

BACKGROUND AND PLACES OF INTEREST:

Dalton in Furness

Dalton was the ancient capital of Furness and in medieval times was the judicial and economic centre serving the nearby monastic community of Furness Abbey. The abbot also built Furness Castle, a massive defensive pele tower in the 14th century, which is now owned by the National Trust. An exhibition (open Saturday afternoons only) commemorates the life of George Romney, the famous portrait painter, who was born in the town in 1734 and lies buried in the churchyard of St Mary's close to the castle. The town boasts a fine market place, interesting buildings and a choice of cafés and pubs. The South Lakeland Wild Animal Park (open daily) lies just to the north of the town on the minor road to Ireleth.

Furness Abbey

Set in the evocative-sounding Vale of Deadly
Nightshade, these deeply romantic red sandstone
ruins are the remains of what was one of the
richest Cistercian abbeys in England, once owning
lands throughout Cumbria and becoming
extremely prosperous from the area's mineral
wealth and extensive woodland. Built largely in the
12th century, but with many later additions, the
splendid transept, choir and western tower still
stand at their original height. Above fine arches
are the remains of the great dormitory, at 57m in
length the largest monastic dormitory in England.
The ruins, now owned and managed by English
Heritage, are open daily in the summer months,
but closed on Mondays and Tuesdays between the
end of October and the beginning of April.

Roa Island

Technically, this little offshore island is a tombolo,
an island now connected to the mainland by sandy
sediments moved by the wave action of the sea.
The Furness Railway Co consolidated the process
by building a causeway carrying its railway line to
a pier at which steamers could arrive to disembark
their passengers from Fleetwood for Barrow and
the Lake District. An impressive new lifeboat
station now stands at the waterfront. A ferry boat
can be taken across Piel Channel to the tiny Piel
Island where, in the 14th century, Furness Abbey
monks built a defensive castle. There is also a pub
on the island whose licensee is 'crowned' King of
Piel, and there is a wildlife sanctuary close by. The
ferry to Piel Island operates at weekends and
during school holidays in the summer months —
telephone the ferry operator on 01229 835809 for
full information.

The Furness Coast Road

This scenic road along the coast of Morecambe
Bay offers an alternative route to the busy A590
between Ulverston and Barrow, with panoramic
views over the bay and down the west coast as far
as Blackpool Tower. The road was built as part of a
major employment project for local shipyard
workers in the 1930s.

Gleaston Water Mill

On the outskirts of the village is Gleaston Water
Mill, an 18th century working corn mill which has
a café selling local produce. The mill is open daily
— Mondays excepted during the summer;
Mondays and Tuesdays excepted during the
winter. At Gleaston Castle, close by, a farmhouse is
now set incongruously amongst the castle ruins.

Great Urswick and Little Urswick

Ancient burial chambers in the form of a mound
are within walking distance of these villages.
Urswick Tarn is a small lake, attractively situated
in a fold of the hills.

Ulverston
For details see Route 22.

Above: Furness Abbey.

Starting Point: Dalton in Furness station. There is a one- to two-hourly rail service from Preston, Lancaster, Carnforth and Barrow with some services also from Manchester. Sunday service is limited to afternoons. Motorists should park at Ulverston station and take the train to Dalton.

Finishing/Return Point: Ulverston as above.

Distance: 32km (20 miles).

Time: $3^1/_2$ hours.

Map: OS Landranger 96: Barrow in Furness & South Lakeland.

Surfaces and Gradients: The route is hilly for the first 6km ($3^3/_4$ miles) between Dalton and Roose. The rest of the ride is in undulating country with mostly gentle gradients; there are long, level stretches along the coast.

Traffic Conditions: Traffic can be busy between Dalton and Furness Abbey. The coast road (A5087) has moderate flows of traffic.

Facilities:
Cafés: Dalton, Ulverston, Gleaston Watermill.
Pubs: Dalton, Ulverston, Great Urswick, Little Urswick, Rampside, Roa Island, Piel Island.
Shops: Dalton, Ulverston, Great Urswick.
WCs: Dalton, Ulverston, Roosebeck, Roa Island.
Tourist Information: Barrow, Ulverston.

ROUTE INSTRUCTIONS:
From Dalton station turn right (crossing over the railway if arriving from Barrow) and take the road which follows the railway, before climbing up the hill. Meeting another road, turn left and take this road through the estate to the cross-roads. Turn right and follow this to the next road, then turn left and go down the hill to the roundabout. Using the green bike lane, follow this main road until a stone gateway over a narrow lane appears on the left. Take this road as it drops down into the valley and passes Furness Abbey.

Follow the road round the abbey before it climbs out of the valley to emerge at a triangular junction. Turn right and follow the lane as it descends to the railway, before climbing up again to pass another estate. Follow the road until the T-junction

and turn right to go down to the roundabout. Turn left on to the A5087 and follow this for 4km ($2^1/_2$ miles) to Rampside, turning right at the roundabout for Roa Island. Follow the road down to Roa Island.

To continue the ride, return on the same road to Rampside. From Rampside rejoin the A5087 coast road and follow it for the next 4 km ($2^1/_2$ miles) until the road moves inland slightly and begins to climb. Turn off left for Gleaston on a lane which goes up and over a fairly steep hill. At Gleaston turn right where small brown signs indicate the water mill. The lane passes the mill and, shortly afterwards, Gleaston Castle. Turn left at the next junction by Scales, take the next right, then go left for Little Urswick. Continue past Urswick Tarn through Great Urswick and follow the road up out of the shallow valley. Turn right at the crossroads and take the next left.

Follow this lane; as it gradually descends an estate appears on the right side of the road. Continue down to the crossroads; turn left as the road dips and rises and enters an older part of town. Ulverston station appears on the left; continue on the road for Ulverston town centre, crossing with care over the busy A590.

ROUTE 24
FURNESS PENINSULA:
DALTON, ROOSE TO ROA ISLAND AND ULVERSTON

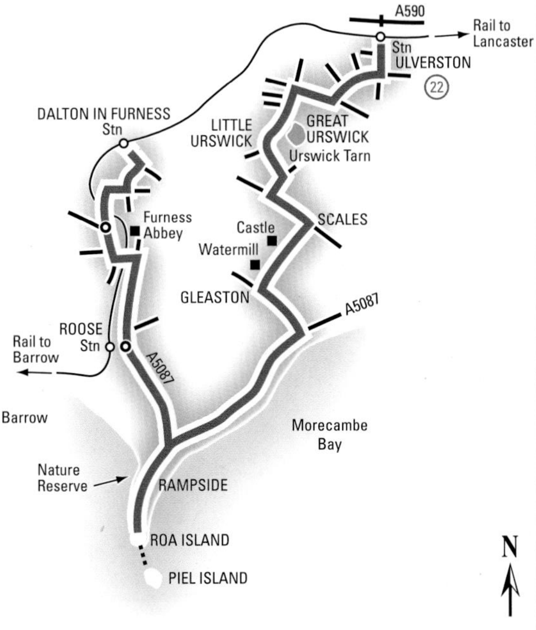

🚲 ROUTE 25

ALONG THE SOLWAY COAST I — ALLONBY AND SILLOTH: MARYPORT TO WIGTON

The Solway coast is one of the most beautiful and least discovered parts of Cumbria, as rich in history and heritage as it is in natural beauty. There is no better way of exploring the Solway than by bicycle. This ride from the old port of Maryport follows the coastal road northwards to take full advantage of the marvellous views across the Solway Firth to Criffel and the Dumfriesshire and Galloway hills, passing through the old seaside resort of Allonby to Silloth and Skinburness, before following the network of quiet lanes across the Cumbria plain via Holm Cultram Abbey in Abbey Town to Wigton.

Below: The war memorial and green at Silloth.

BACKGROUND AND PLACES OF INTEREST

Solway Coast AONB
The Solway Coast AONB extends from north of Maryport to Rockcliffe near Carlisle. Its 115sq km covers mainly coastal scenery, but includes extensive areas of salt marsh and sand dune further inland around Bowness. The area is protected because of its superb coastal land and seascapes — there are long views over dunes and marsh and the Solway Firth to the Scottish coast — as well as for the richness of its marine and birdlife in its fragile ecosystem.

Maryport
Maryport was established by local industrialist Humphrey Senhouse in the estuary of the little River Ellen in 1749 and named after his wife Mary. For many years it was a busy little port, mainly exporting coal from a series of rail-served docks and wharves. It was also a fishing port, a function that continues. In recent years it has been rebuilt and redeveloped as a marina, its old docks

restored with a new housing and leisure development around the wharf area, including a maritime museum, an historic steamship dock and the remarkable Senhouse Roman Museum on Sea Brows with its collection of Roman altars, many from the nearby Roman town of Alauna, once the headquarters of the Roman coastal defence system of fortlets and signal stations that reached Hadrian's Wall at Bowness.

Crosscanonby Salt Pans
From medieval times the brine from the Solway was dried in great salt pans to produce sea salt, a precious product used to preserve food. The salt pans at Crosscanonby date from the 17th century and are accessible from a lay-by at the roadside, having been preserved as an industrial monument.

Allonby
In the 18th century Allonby was as regarded as highly as Scarborough as a seaside resort, with an attractive grassy foreshore leading down to the sandy bay. It was also an important area for shrimping, herring fishing and kipper smoking.

Among several interesting buildings are a colonnaded building which was once a bathing house, where sea water was warmed for visitors, and the Ship Inn, where the two great Victorian writers and friends, Charles Dickens and Wilkie Collins, stayed in the 1850s.

Silloth-on-Solway
Silloth takes it name from the monks of nearby Holm Cultram Abbey who stored their grain in barns known in northern dialect as 'laithes'; hence 'sea-laithes', because they were by the sea, became corrupted to 'Silloth'. It is a quiet, sheltered seaside resort which has kept its Victorian charm, with cobbled streets, handsome buildings and glorious sea views from across its extensive greens. There is a good choice of accommodation in the town, ideal for anyone planning to combine Routes 25 and 26 along the Solway coast.

Skinburness
A former fishing village which, in medieval times was a market town and port where Edward I's navy waited before attacking the Scots in 1299. Grune Point, a spit of shingle beyond the village, is now a Site of Special Scientific Interest noted for its birdlife. The road eastwards from Skinburness on this ride follows an ancient sea dyke.

Above: A doorway at Holm Cultram Abbey.

Abbeytown

Abbeytown parish church is the surviving portion of Holm Cultram Abbey, a once-powerful Cistercian abbey founded by Prince Henry, son of King David I of Scotland, when for a time this part of Cumbria belonged to Scotland. The abbey's colourful and often troubled history includes a period when the monks had to pay 'protection money' of £200 per year — a considerable sum in those days — to Scottish raiders in return for not being destroyed. The portion that remains is the former nave of the abbey church to which a fine gateway was added in 1730.

Wigton

This busy little ancient market town, now dominated to the west by industry and a new bypass, has had a royal market charter since 1262. Most of the town centre is now a conservation area with many attractive buildings, several dating back to the 18th century when the town flourished as a centre for the weaving of cotton and linen (many weavers' cottages remain), as well as for dyeing, printing and tanning using readily available local water power. The handsome Memorial Fountain in the market place was erected by local merchant George Moore in memory of his wife.

Starting Point: Maryport railway station on the West Cumbrian line. There are trains from Carlisle, Workington and Whitehaven every 1-2 hours (less frequently on Sundays), and approximately 5/6 trains per day through to Barrow. Motorists should park in Wigton, take an outward train to Maryport, and return to their vehicles by cycle.

Finishing/Return Point: Wigton station as above.

Distance: 45km (28 miles).

Time: 4 hours.

Maps: OS Landranger 85: Carlisle & Solway Firth; 89: West Cumbria.

Surfaces and Gradients: The route uses good tarmac surfaces throughout, with a few gradients which are generally very easy, being no more than 20-30m.

Traffic Conditions: There is a very busy unavoidable section of about 1km ($^1/_2$ mile) on the A596 out of Maryport then moderate traffic of mainly tourist cars along the B5300 to Silloth. It is quiet through Skinburness, then the 2.5km ($1^1/_2$ miles) along the B5302 is on a fairly busy and fast road, before you return on quiet lanes directly to Wigton station.

Facilities:
Cafés: Maryport, Allonby, Silloth, Wigton.
Pubs: Maryport, Allonby, Silloth, Abbey Town, Wigton.
Shops: Maryport, Allonby, Silloth, Abbey Town, Wigton.
WCs: Maryport, Allonby, Silloth, Wigton.
Tourist Information: Maryport, Silloth.

Below: The Scottish hills across the Solway Firth.

ROUTE 25
SOLWAY COAST I

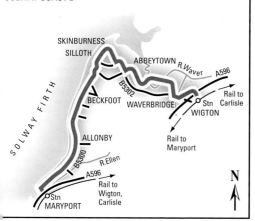

ROUTE INSTRUCTIONS:

From Maryport station go straight ahead, crossing a minor road and keeping ahead to Curzon Street in the town centre. Turn right past the pelican crossing then first left up Senhouse Street (one-way), the town's main street. This ascends a short hillock and then descends to the harbour area with its wharves, cafés, pubs, well-signed Maritime Museum and other heritage attractions.

Return the way you came, turning left at the one-way system at Senhouse Street up High Street, then take the first right which leads back into the main A596 road by the parish church. Turn left for just under a kilometre (¹/₂ mile) along this unpleasantly busy trunk road, climbing steadily to the junction with the B5300 signed to Silloth. Turn left here. Most of the traffic now disappears, although there is still enough local and tourist traffic to require care. This is more than compensated for by the increasingly superb views across the dunes and marram grass to the Solway Firth and the Scottish coast and mountains on your left. After 3km (2 miles) you pass the turning to Crosscanonby; note the lay-by and entrance to Crosscanonby salt pans on the right.

Continue for another 3km (2 miles) to the little seaside town of Allonby, which is worth spending time to explore.

The route continues along the gently undulating B5300, past the village of Mawbray and the scattered hamlet of Beckfoot, using the spire of Silloth church as a landmark as you approach. The main road turns right beyond Blitterlees, then curves left to cross the bridge over the long defunct Carlisle–Silloth railway line and left again into the long, cobbled Eden Street which leads to the seafront and small dock area (with occasional

Right: Holm Cultram Abbey, Abbeytown.

heavy lorries, so take care). Turn right along the cobbled Criffel Street which forms the main promenade, go past the tourist information centre, shops and café, with a pleasant waterside park and amusement arcade on the left. Keep ahead along Criffel Street towards Skinburness; the road soon (thankfully for most cyclists) becomes smooth tarmac, with the shoreline on the left and suburban houses to the right. Keep ahead on the main road into Skinburness, turning right past the grand Skinburness Hotel which leads directly over a cattle grid and follows an ancient sea dyke, with cows grazing literally on the road.

Follow this road across the open pastures until, over another cattle grid, it curves round Hartlaw Farm to join the busy B5302 road. Go left here, taking care with the often fast-moving traffic, and follow the road past Calvo Farm for 2km (1¹/₄ miles), before reaching a large double-crossing. Now take the second lane on the left towards Brownrigg and Border. Follow it to a T-junction where you turn right, alongside the River Waver, and head past Winding Banks to Abbey Town, back on the B5302. Turn left again through the village, keeping ahead on the B5307 towards Newton Arlosh and soon passing the superb red sandstone abbey church of Holm Cultram. Keep in the same direction for another 2km (1¹/₄ miles) to the hamlet of Raby, where you take the narrow lane on the right which passes low-lying fields, crossing over a stream towards the hamlet of Lessonhall. Go right here, back to the B5302 at Waverbridge. Turn left, and after 200m turn left again along a minor road signed to Aikhead and Station Hill which climbs gently, passing pylons and a cemetery before entering the outskirts of Wigton. If you are going to the station, do not go down to the very busy bypass, which has an awkward and dangerous right turn across the speeding traffic, but bear left along a cul-de-sac road which leads to an enclosed footpath (walking is required) that crosses to the ramped footbridge over the bypass directly ahead to the rear entrance to Wigton railway station. If you are going into Wigton town centre with its many facilities, there is direct access along a road from the south entrance of the station.

ALONG THE SOLWAY COAST II — BOWNESS AND BURGH BY SANDS: WIGTON TO CARLISLE

This ride continues Route 25 along the Solway coast, starting from Wigton then following quiet roads along the extended shoreline. The ride gives every opportunity to enjoy the northern end of the Solway Coast AONB, which also includes the western end of the Hadrian's Wall World Heritage Site. The route calls at some unusual and attractive villages, before finally finding a reasonably comfortable way through the traffic into the great border city of Carlisle.

BACKGROUND AND PLACES OF INTEREST:

Solway Coast AONB
This section of the Solway Coast AONB (see also Route 25) is remarkable not just for its fine coastal views but also for its salt marsh rich in birdlife and its raised mires (peat bogs), which are amongst the most extensive in Britain and are host to many rare plants and much insect life. Particularly noteworthy are the flocks of pink-footed geese which arrive on the coast in late September and return to the Arctic in early spring.

Wigton
See Route 25.

Bowness-on-Solway
Bowness actually marked the western end of Hadrian's Wall (and of the Hadrian's Wall National Trail) although very little of the fort of Maia, which once stood here, is visible. The reason is that so much masonry and stones from the ruins were used in the walls of the church and local cottages of this little fishing village. The estuary or firth is about 1.5km (1 mile) wide here, and Bowness is the last place westwards where it could still be crossed on foot or horseback (albeit over a somewhat dangerous ford) which is why the Romans built their defensive fort here. What is visible, however, are the remains of the embankment of the Solway Viaduct which provided a rail link between Cumbria and Dumfriesshire between 1869 and 1921. Originally built to carry West Cumbrian iron ore to the Lanarkshire steelworks, it also carried passengers for a while.

This was always an area which suffered from border raids, which were still continuing here as late as 1626 when some marauding Scots stole Bowness church bells. In retaliation two bells were seized by Bowness men from Dornock and Middlebie in Dumfriesshire. The area also specialises in 'haaf net' fishing in which fishermen stand side by side in the channel holding out nets between giant wooden frames to catch salmon with the ebbing tide.

Port Carlisle
This old harbour on the Solway was also once served by canal and railway. In the early 19th century, when the only alternative to water was horse transport, Port Carlisle was planned as a faster link for goods and people from Carlisle to

Below: On a minor road near Bowness, with a high tide warning.

Inset: A First North Western diesel multiple-unit leaving Wigton station.

reach other English and Irish ports as well as even further afield. The US President Woodrow Wilson's mother, who came from Carlisle, emigrated from here. To improve and reduce the costs of freight carriage, the 11-mile-long Carlisle Canal was opened to Port Carlisle in 1823 but the railway eventually took over and track was laid in the canal bed in 1853. The line soon became famous for horse-drawn carts or 'dandies' which travelled along it between Port Carlisle and Drumburgh — the last surviving one is in the National Railway Museum in York.

Drumburgh

The name of this village is believed to mean 'bog of the bitterns'. Drumburgh castle was built by Thomas, Lord Dacre, and rebuilt in 1681 with stones from the nearby Roman fort. Recently restored, the castle is now a farmhouse.

Cardurnock

A Roman fortlet once stood here, the first in a chain of small forts and signal towers linked to Hadrian's Wall along the Solway. Cardurnock was famed for its damson orchards, the remnants of which can be seen beside old farmhouses.

Burgh by Sands

It was discovered in the 1970s that the Romans had made their mark here long before Hadrian, when a fort dating from AD95 was discovered south of the village of Burgh by Sands. The church, built using Roman masonry, dates from 1180 and is an excellent example of a fortified church, with small windows and $7^1/_2$ ft-thick walls. In 1307 the militant English monarch Edward I died on Burgh Marsh while leading troops against the Scots. His body lay in state in Burgh church whilst homage was paid to him. A monument in the form of a tall weatherbeaten stone obelisk stands where Edward died in the lonely sands and the track to reach it is signed from the centre of Burgh.

The Cumberland Bird of Prey Centre is at Thurstonfield Lough, 2km ($1^1/_4$ mile) south of Burgh by Sands.

Starting Point: Wigton railway station. Trains operate approximately hourly (infrequently on Sundays) between Carlisle, Wigton and Whitehaven. Motorists should park in Carlisle, take the train out and cycle back to their vehicle — although on Sundays it would make more sense to park in Wigton and return on one of the few afternoon trains.

Finishing/Return Point: Carlisle railway station.

Distance: 52km (32¹/₃ miles).

Time: 4¹/₂ hours.

Map: OS Landranger 85: Carlisle & Solway Firth.

Surfaces and Gradients: This route is a very easy ride with occasional short, gentle climbs and long, flat stretches.

Traffic Conditions: The ride is very quiet as far as Burgh by Sands, then the traffic becomes heavier as you approach Carlisle. A bike lane in Carlisle avoids the worst traffic along the city ring road. The ride out of Wigton follows a less direct route than the road to Kirkbride, which, although narrow, is used as a dangerous racetrack by local drivers.

Facilities:
Cafés: Wigton, Carlisle.
Pubs: Wigton, Bowness-on-Solway, Port Carlisle, Burgh by Sands, Carlisle.
Shops: Wigton, Carlisle.
WCs: Wigton, Carlisle.
Tourist Information: Carlisle.

ROUTE INSTRUCTIONS:
From Wigton station (the Whitehaven/Barrow platform) follow the road out by the exit and then turn left to walk along the pavement under the rail bridge. Follow the path up and over the bridge crossing the bypass. If you are starting from the Carlisle platform, take the exit on to the bridge over the bypass.

Turn right on to the tarmac path and follow this round until it joins the road at the top of the slope. Continue straight ahead as it descends. Just before a sharp bend take the right turn (care is required) and follow this lane until it ends at a T-junction. Turn right by the farm (signed Aikton) and follow this lane as it dips and climbs, before turning left, signed for Gamelsby. Follow this narrow lane through Gamelsby Biglands and Wampool. At the Laythes turn right and then

left to go in between the farm buildings. Go straight ahead at the next cross-roads and at the next junction continue on the lane to Anthorn. The road now follows the edge of a peninsula in the Solway Firth with spectacular views across to the Scottish hills to the north and to the south the peaks of the Skiddaw massif of the Lake District.

The lane follows the coast, in some sections at a very low level which may be subject to inundation under a very high tide. Follow the lane through Bowness, Port Carlisle and Burgh by Sands through to the edge of Carlisle where the B5307 is joined. Continue as far as the junction with the main dual carriageway, taking the bike lane which appears on the left.

Follow the bike lane over the bridge, and by the castle take the underpass to cross under the ring road as far as the pedestrian precinct. Follow the precinct (cyclists must dismount) through to English Street and cross by the lights, continuing straight ahead along the pavement by foot to the railway station.

Above: The coast road on Solway, near Bowness.

ROUTE 26
ALONG THE SOLWAY COAST Ⅱ
WIGTON - CARLISLE

EAST OF EDEN: APPLEBY TO LANGWATHBY

The Eden Valley, with its gently undulating, richly fertile countryside and network of virtually traffic-free lanes, is perfect cycling country. This ride from the lovely old town of Appleby, which still likes to call itself Appleby in Westmorland, takes in no less than 11 characteristic Eden Valley red sandstone villages. But what dominates this ride is the spectacular, ever-changing backcloth of the North Pennine hills immediately to the east, which, when lit by an afternoon or winter sun, make a dramatic feature. The outlines of the Lake District mountains are also visible to the west at several points along this ride.

Above: Long Meg and her Daughters.

BACKGROUND AND PLACES OF INTEREST:

The Eden Valley

The River Eden is remarkable, being one of the few rivers of any size in England to flow northwards. From its source high on Lunds Fell in the Yorkshire Dales it flows to its estuary in the Solway Firth, west of Carlisle. The dark red sandstone which gives the Eden villages, barns and field walls their characteristic colour is part of a huge horseshoe of Permian and Triassic sandstone laid down more than 200 million years ago, that extends from St Bees Head around the Lake District and gives this landscape a real feel of the Scottish borders. It owes its colour to the presence of iron oxide in the rock. The three great outlying conical hills of Murton Pike, Dufton Pike and Knock Pike, notable features on the early part of the ride, are the result of a geological accident in which layers of ancient rock were thrust up between the red sandstone and the main Pennine escarpment to produce dramatic, rounded hills.

Dufton

Until the first part of the 19th century Dufton was a mining village, in which lead was worked from mines in the nearby hills. On the Pennine Way, it is now one of the most popular villages in the Eden Valley, with fine, open views. Its large village green, complete with a sandstone pump, is surrounded by attractive 18th and 19th century houses and farms, and a cosy village inn.

St Cuthbert's Church

The charming little church of St Cuthbert, passed on the route, lies almost half-way between Dufton and its neighbouring village of Knock. Its secluded location is almost certainly an ancient Christian site, even though its parish registers go back to only the 16th century, whilst the existing buildings date from the 1780s.

Milburn

There are few more delightful, unspoiled villages in Eden than Milburn. It is a superb example of a Border defence village, built around a large village green which in times of marauding Scots in the 14th century could be used for the protection of cattle and sheep, and other goods and chattels. It has an impressive maypole.

Melmerby

This village lies at the bottom of Hartside Pass which carries the main A686 road high across the North Pennines between Penrith and Alston. It is also on the popular C2C cycle route. As well as a pub and a shop, it has the celebrated Melmerby Village Bakery, noted throughout the north for its home-made organic bread and cakes and its wholefood café. Cyclists are always welcome.

Gamlesby and Glassonby

Gamlesby is an extended village with a large village green, complete with the remains of stocks and an unusual red sandstone church. Glassonby is a smaller village, noted for its church dating from 1200 known as Addingham Church, after a long-vanished neighbouring village. The church has 15th century bells and some remarkable carved stones.

Long Meg and her Daughters

Overlooking one of the largest Neolithic circles in the country, Long Meg is a 5m-high megalith. This column of Penrith sandstone is decorated with cup and ring markings and is possibly 4,500 years old. The four corners face the four points of the compass, four 'daughter' boulders stand close to her in a square formation and there are a total of 66 stones in the great oval. The exact purpose of the stones is unclear, though it is interesting to note that the setting of the midwinter sun on the winter solstice is exactly aligned with the centre of the circle and with Long Meg herself.

Little Salkeld Mill

A working water mill, Little Salkeld grinds and sells a variety of stone-ground flours and other cereal products in its shop. A café is available with products from the mill (open Mondays to Fridays only).

Langwathby

One of the larger villages in the Eden Valley, Langwathby has an extensive village green (still used for maypole dancing each spring) which is probably medieval in origin. The Shepherds' Inn on the green was originally known as the Highland Laddie from associations with Scottish drovers using the road that passed through the village to drive cattle from Scotland. The station café, Brief Encounter, has a good reputation for home-made cakes, lunches and teas and is open from Easter until the end of October.

Below: Dufton village.

Starting Point: Appleby station, on the Settle–Carlisle line. Services operate every two or three hours on weekdays (less frequently on Sundays) from Carlisle and Settle. On summer Sundays there are direct Lancashire Dales Rail trains from Blackburn, Preston and Blackpool. Motorists should park at Langwathby station (parking for rail customers only) or Appleby and either cycle back to their vehicle or take the train back from Langwathby.

Finishing/Return Point: Langwathby station.

Distance: 37km (23 miles).

Time: 4¹/₂ hours.

Maps: OS Landranger 90: Penrith & Keswick; 91: Appleby.

Surfaces and Gradients: The route is on good surfaces throughout. There is one steep gradient between Appleby and Dufton, otherwise the gradients are moderate.

Traffic Conditions: Traffic is generally very light, although expect more local traffic at weekends and some tourist traffic during the summer.

Facilities:
Cafés: Appleby, Melmerby, Little Salkeld (Water Mill — Mondays to Fridays only), Langwathby.
Pubs: Appleby, Dufton, Milburn (Stag Inn 500m before the village), Ousby, Melmerby, Langwathby.
Shops: Appleby, Dufton, Knock (at Silverband 600m north of village), Melmerby, Langwathby.
WCs: Appleby (station and town), Dufton, Langwathby (station).
Tourist Information: Appleby.
Youth Hostel: Dufton.

ROUTE INSTRUCTIONS:
If arriving by train at Appleby from the Settle direction, turn sharp right outside the station entrance by the Midland Hotel and right again under the railway bridge. If coming from Langwathby or Carlisle, take the pedestrian entrance from the platform and turn right into the same road. Cross the level crossing of the defunct Barnard Castle–Tebay Stainmoor Railway by the old Appleby East station (hopefully, the line will soon be reopened between Appleby and Warcop), heading up towards the main A66 Appleby bypass.

Above: Little Salkeld water mill.

Follow the lane right as it descends to a tunnel on the left, going under the bypass. Turn left beyond the tunnel, returning parallel with the A66, already with superb views of Murton Fell and Dufton Fell and the North Pennines to your right.

At the feeder road from the bypass to Appleby keep ahead and go to the road junction with the Dufton road, turning right, away from Appleby. Keep ahead past the junction to Long Marton and Brampton, before descending to the bridge over Trout Beck then taking the very steep climb by Dufton Wood. There is a descent before the road swings left and climbs quite sharply into Dufton village, which is a good place to pause to enjoy its fine green and open views.

From Dufton take the road at the end of the village which bears right, going downhill towards Knock. You soon reach St Cuthbert's Church on a hillock on the right, which is accessible by a path. Keep ahead for Knock, going through the village towards Milburn. This lane turns sharp left after 1km by Milburn Grange, heading westwards to join a slightly wider lane past the Stag Inn which heads northwards to Milburn. Take the fork right to see the lovely village of Milburn with its fine green. Pass along the end of the green to the next cross-roads, turning right (again northwestwards), this time to Blencarn, which is another pleasant if less spectacular village.

Turn left in Blencarn, but after 150m bear right towards Skirwith on an attractive road. Skirwith is a linear village along the steep valley of the Skirwith Beck, which you cross twice. Keep going in the same direction up the hill, bearing right at the next junction towards Ousby and Melmerby. Ousby is a small settlement — go through the village following the Melmerby signs, bearing right by the evocatively named Fox & Old Snug Inn towards Melmerby.

Melmerby is a larger village on the fairly busy A686 Penrith–Alston road which you should cross with care. The pub and shop are on the right, Melmerby bakery and restaurant are on the left, but your route is uphill to the right, although as the main road bends right keep straight ahead along the quiet lane to Gamblesby. Keep straight ahead through this rather scattered red sandstone village (this section also carries the C2C route) but bear left at the end of the village following the signs to Glassonby and Little Salkeld and keep right where the road forks towards Glassonby on a slow and steady climb.

Glassonby is another village on a hillside. Bear left up and through the village following the Little Salkeld and Langwathby signs. Just beyond the village a cul-de-sac lane on the right leads to Addingham Church. If you decide to visit the church, return to the main road and continue to a cross-roads, turning right towards Little Salkeld and Langwathby. This road soon begins a pleasant descent past Tarn House Farm. Do not go too fast otherwise you will miss the next junction where an old-fashioned sign on the lane on the right directs you to the 'Druids Circle'. This narrow lane takes you to the impressive Neolithic stone circle of Long Meg and her Daughters.

Return the same way to the Langwathby road, where now a sharp, curving descent takes you into Little Salkeld, where the water mill is passed by the bridge over the stream. There is a short ascent out of Little Salkeld and under the railway bridge carrying the Settle–Carlisle line, then the route goes alongside the railway to emerge finally at Langwathby's large village green. Keep ahead alongside the green to join the busy A686 for a short uphill section (cross with care here) to Langwathby station. If you are travelling in the southbound direction, give yourself time after tea and cakes to go under the bridge and along the grassy track at the rear to the southbound platform entrance.

ROUTE 27
EAST OF EDEN

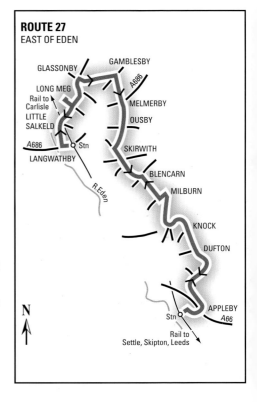

THE EDEN GORGE: BRAMPTON TO ARMATHWAITE AND LAZONBY

This ride follows the cusp of the North Pennines into the wooded Eden Gorge. Starting from Brampton station, the route calls in at nearby Talkin Tarn, a local beauty spot, before taking a mid-level route across to the Eden Valley, following the river upstream to Armathwaite. Climbing out of Armathwaite, on the opposite side of the river, the route runs above the dramatic Eden Gorge where open views of the highest of the North Pennines appear. The final descent leads into the village of Lazonby, a fine village built from the local red sandstone.

BACKGROUND AND PLACES OF INTEREST:

Talkin Tarn Country Park
This very pleasant lake covering 26 hectares has its origins in the last Ice Age, and is currently sustained by underwater springs. The tarn is now a popular country park with boating, cycling, walking, nature trails, picnic sites and fishing on offer, and there is also a café serving refreshments.

Armathwaite
The central feature of this attractive village is a fine sandstone bridge which crosses the River Eden, from where there is a view of Armathwaite Castle on the riverside, a former four-storey pele tower extended in the 18th century (not open to the public). Nearby are the famous Nunnery Walks along the riverside.

Lazonby
Lazonby is a lovely red sandstone village, with a fine village green, a shop, a pub, an attractive duck pond and a swimming pool adjacent to the River Eden, which is crossed by an impressive stone bridge that links Lazonby with its attractive twin village, Kirkoswald. The village is noted for its regular sheep sales, the largest held in the north of England, and as the home of a noted Cumbrian bakery.

Below: Armathwaite Hall and the River Eden.

Inset: Muscovy ducks on Talkin Tarn.

Starting Point: Brampton railway station. There are approximately 5/6 train services per day (Sundays included) between Carlisle, Haltwhistle and Newcastle on the Tyne Valley line, although there are 2-3hr gaps between some services so check train times carefully before travelling. Motorists should park in Carlisle and catch the outward train to Brampton, returning from Lazonby or Armathwaite.

Finishing/Return Points: Either Armathwaite or Lazonby & Kirkoswald stations on the Settle-Carlisle Line. There are trains every 2-3 hours to Carlisle or Settle; less frequently on Sundays.

Distance: 17km (10^1/$_2$ miles) to Armathwaite; 27km (16^3/$_4$ miles) to Lazonby.

Time: Armathwaite 2 hours; Lazonby & Kirkoswald 3 hours.

Maps: OS Landranger 86: Haltwhistle & Bewcastle; (also 90: Penrith & Keswick for the last mile, so not really necessary).

Surfaces and Gradients: The ride is on good tarmac surfaces throughout. Gradients are generally moderate, being relatively easy for the main part of the route between Brampton and Armathwaite, with a steady, steeper climb of 110m out of Armathwaite.

Traffic Conditions: Traffic is generally light.

Below: Lazonby Bridge.

Facilities:
Cafés: Talkin Tarn Country Park.
Pubs: Castle Carrock, Armathwaite, Lazonby.
Shops: Castle Carrock, Armathwaite, Lazonby.
WCs: Talkin Tarn.
Tourist Information: Brampton.
Youth Hostel: Carlisle.
Cycle Hire: Brampton, Talkin Tarn.

ROUTE INSTRUCTIONS:

Take the exit from the Carlisle-bound platform at Brampton station (if you are travelling from Carlisle, use the footbridge). Turn right on to the lane and head for the B6413. Turn left and cross the railway by the level crossing, taking the next left for Talkin Tarn.

Leave Talkin Tarn by the same road and return to the B6413, following this road as far as Castle Carrock. Leaving Castle Carrock at the left-hand bend, take the lane straight ahead, signed for Armathwaite.

Continue along this lane for 8km (5 miles) and take the turn-off for Armathwaite which is on the lower part of a descent into the Eden Valley. Follow this lane as it drops to the riverside and then recovers some height before emerging at a T-junction. Turn right and cross the River Eden into Armathwaite, turning left at the next junction. (If returning from Armathwaite, the station is signed from the village centre.)

Follow the road signed for Penrith, which soon climbs, taking the left turn to Penrith after going under the railway bridge, and take the next left for Lazonby. Follow the lane as it makes a steady climb above the Eden Gorge and then drops down into Lazonby (ignore the turn-offs). Once in the village, at the T-junction turn right for the station; the station entrances are on both sides of the bridge, the nearer for southbound (Leeds) trains, the further for Carlisle trains.

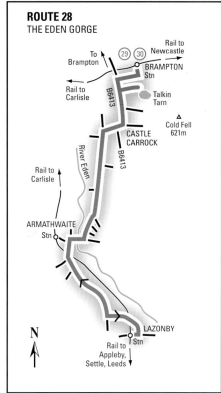

ROUTE 28
THE EDEN GORGE

🚲 ROUTE 29

ROAMING THE ROMAN WALL TO BIRDOSWALD AND LANERCOST PRIORY: BRAMPTON CIRCULAR

The Cumbrian section of Hadrian's Wall, with its protected landscape corridor, goes through countryside of grandeur, wildness and beauty. This circular ride from Brampton drops down from Brampton, crosses over the river and then takes you up through Walton. The route continues through rolling pasture land just north of the wall,

Below: Irthing Gorge.

calling at the Roman fort museum at Birdoswald, then goes along the wall above the Irthing Valley before dropping down by Lanercost Priory, continuing past Naworth Castle and returning to Brampton.

BACKGROUND AND PLACES OF INTEREST:

Hadrian's Wall

One of the most spectacular remains of Roman civilisation in northern Europe, the 117km-long (73-mile) Hadrian's Wall is now a World Heritage Site. Visitors can explore the splendours of its surviving sections, including several forts and milecastles, as well as the countryside of bleak grandeur through which it passes, much of which is now also protected as part of the world heritage corridor.

Brampton

This attractive old market town was the headquarters of Bonnie Prince Charlie during his siege of Carlisle in 1745; a plaque on a black and white building in High Cross Street in the town centre commemorates the fact. Also in the town centre is the fine octagonal Moot Hall built in 1817, and a church noted for its 19th century Burne-Jones windows, as well as a choice of pubs, cafés and shops.

Birdoswald Roman Fort Museum

This is the site of one of the major Roman forts on Hadrian's Wall. The museum, itself in an interesting building, houses an outstanding exhibition of Roman soldiers' life, based on considerable excavations in the area. The remains of the fort overlook a spectacular gorge cut into the hillside by the River Irthing. Hadrian's Wall is particularly well preserved in this area.

Banks Turret

A well-preserved Turf Wall turret along the Roman wall can be seen beside the road. There are also the remains of a signal tower close by.

Lanercost Priory and Lanercost Church

Lanercost Priory was founded in 1166 by the Norman lords of nearby Gilsland who wanted to set up a house of prayer and chose the Augustinian canons to establish the priory. The priory had land deeds recorded in the cartulary (monastery register book) in the 13th and 14th centuries and was used as a base by Edward I in his punitive wars with the Scots. In 1306/7 his seal was brought to Lanercost, making it temporarily the centre of English government. After the defeat of the English forces at Bannockburn in 1315, the priory suffered greatly in raids by the Scots. It was finally disbanded at the Dissolution, but in 1740 the ruined nave was restored for use as the village parish church. The present church is notable for its fine William Morris glass. Admission to the church and its exhibition is free, whilst a charge is made for the priory.

Naworth Castle

This magnificent border castle dates back to 1335 when an earlier fortified manor house or pele tower was developed into an important stronghold by Lord Dacre to keep out the marauding Scots. The castle was used for the setting of Sir Walter Scott's poem The Lay of the Last Minstrel. It is open to the public in the summer months, and has a superb great hall hung with French tapestries and guarded by heraldic beasts. There is a 116ft-long gallery with a major collection of paintings belonging to the Earl of Carlisle, the present owner.

Above: The East Gate at Birdoswald Fort, Hadrian's Wall. *Cumbria Tourist Board*

Starting and Finishing Point: Brampton railway station. There are approximately 5/6 train services per day (Sundays included) between Carlisle, Haltwhistle and Newcastle on the Tyne Valley line; gaps between some services can be 2-3 hours so check these and your return train times carefully before travelling. Motorists should park in Brampton.

Distance: 34km (21 miles).

Time: 4$^1/_2$ hours.

Map: OS Landranger 86: Haltwhistle & Bewcastle.

Above: Birdoswald, Hadrian's Wall.
Cumbria Tourist Board

Surfaces and Gradients: This ride is on tarmac lanes throughout, which are generally hilly, but with some long level sections. The rider should leave plenty of time for the last part of the ride from Lanercost to Brampton station as there is a long climb at the end.

Traffic Conditions: Traffic is generally light, apart from the A69 which has to be crossed with care.

Facilities:
Cafés: Brampton, Birdoswald Roman Museum.
Pubs: Brampton, Walton.
Shops: Brampton.
WCs: Brampton, Birdoswald Roman Museum.
Tourist Information: Brampton.
Youth Hostels: Greenhead, Carlisle.

Above: Cycling on the road to Birdoswald.

3km (2 miles) the B6318 is met; turn right on to this road and follow it for 8km (5 miles). The Birdoswald turn-off is on the right at the bottom of a steep dip in the road. Follow this lane as it drops and then ascends to the Roman Museum.

From Birdoswald the route continues along the lane following the Roman Wall past Banks Turret. Turn left at the fork to descend steeply into the Irthing Valley, following the valley bottom before Lanercost Priory appears on the left. Continue along the road, bending left to cross the river and climbing steeply up the other bank.

(For Brampton town follow the road over the river and continue along this road up the other bank before a slight descent is made into Brampton.)

Leave Lanercost on the same road to cross the river and immediately take the left turn-off past the bridge to climb steeply through woodland and estate grounds. The road passes Naworth Castle before meeting the A69. With care cross over to the road opposite and continue straight ahead, crossing the railway at the level crossing. Where the A689 is met, turn right and follow it for about 1$\frac{1}{2}$ km (1 mile); turn left for Brampton station.

ROUTE INSTRUCTIONS:

From Brampton station take the exit from the Newcastle-bound platform and follow the lane to the end. Turn left on to the A689 and follow it to the junction with the A69. Go over the slightly staggered junction and continue on the A689 down into Brampton. Passing the green, turn left to continue into the town centre.

Turn right on to the A6071, which descends to the riverside and crosses over by means of a narrow bridge controlled by traffic lights. Shortly afterwards turn right and ascend to the village of Walton. The road bends left; continue on this road, ignoring the left turn-off as it gradually ascends. After

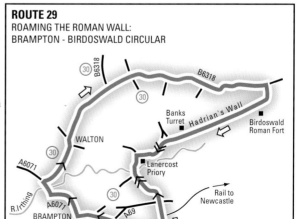

ROUTE 29
ROAMING THE ROMAN WALL:
BRAMPTON - BIRDOSWALD CIRCULAR

BEYOND THE WALL INTO BORDER COUNTRY: BRAMPTON CIRCULAR

This ride through the rolling borderland hills north of Hadrian's Wall explores the little-known northeastern tip of Cumbria. In late medieval times this lawless region was prey to the Scottish raiders known as the Reivers. Crossing the Irthing Valley, the ride goes north to the rough pastures of the upper Lyne Valley below the rolling plateau of this relatively low but exposed part of the northern Pennines. The climb out of Bewcastle offers superb views of the Scottish borders and also westwards to the Lakeland fells. Returning southwards there is an exhilarating descent before you cross the next valley. The route passes the line of Hadrian's Wall before dropping down to Lanercost Priory and into Brampton.

This route could be combined with Route 29 to include Birdoswald Roman Fort if time allows, or the two routes could offer a very attractive weekend break in Reiver country.

BACKGROUND AND PLACES OF INTEREST:

The Reivers

Much of the Border countryside was, during the later Middle Ages, subject to constant raids from marauding gangs of cattle and sheep rustlers. These included the notorious families of Reivers who were able to rob and loot without fear of reprisal because of the remoteness of the countryside, away from the usual forces of law and order. Centuries later, this remains a countryside of old fortified houses and small towns and villages, reflecting the area's unsettled history. The history of this area is graphically told in Carlisle's Tullie House Museum. (See also the Reivers Cycle Route [page 108] from Carlisle through the Borders.)

Brampton

See Route 29.

Above right: Bewcastle Castle.

Inset: Bewcastle Cross.

Walton

This is a very small but attractive village, typical of the Border country, with pleasant cottages, a church, a village green and fine views across the Irthing Valley.

Bewcastle

Bewcastle was the site of a Roman fort from AD122 which was occupied until the fourth century. The original garrison troops were probably Dacian (from what is now Romania), who were based at Birdoswald in the third century. In AD142 the fort was abandoned when the Antonine

Wall was constructed by the Romans further to the north in Scotland, but after their withdrawal back into the Borders the fort was reoccupied in AD163. Amongst the archaeological finds in the village have been silver plaques and bronze letters which are now in Tullie House Museum in Carlisle. It is unknown when Bewcastle Castle was built, but it was first recorded in 1379. In 1401 it was captured by the Scots. There is an exhibition of local archaeological finds and an interpretation of the area's rich history in the Old Barn by the churchyard.

Bewcastle Cross

Standing in Bewcastle churchyard, this superbly decorated Anglo-Saxon monolith, one of the finest of its type in the British Isles, is thought to date from the late seventh to early eighth centuries. The richly carved cross with vines, scrolls, knotwork and runes, and a carving of John the Baptist holding a Holy Lamb, is similar in style to the 'crosses' of Jarrow on Tyneside and Ruthwell in Dumfries & Galloway. It is believed to be some form of victory cross.

Lanercost Priory and Church
See Route 29.

Starting and Finishing Point: Brampton station. Motorists should park in Brampton.

Distance: 46km (28¹/₂ miles).

Time: 4¹/₂ hours.

Map: OS Landranger 86: Haltwhistle & Bewcastle.

Surfaces and Gradients: The ride takes place on tarmac roads throughout. This is a hilly route, with some moderate gradients in places.

Traffic Conditions: The route uses generally quiet roads throughout.

Facilities:
Cafés: Brampton.
Pubs: Brampton, Walton, Bewcastle.
Stores: Brampton.
WCs: Brampton.
Tourist Information: Brampton.
Youth Hostels: Greenhead, Carlisle.

Below: Lyneholmeford.

ROUTE INSTRUCTIONS:

From Brampton station take the exit from the Newcastle-bound platform and follow the lane to the end. Turn left on to the A689 and follow it to the junction with the A69. Go over the slightly staggered junction and continue on the A689 down into Brampton. Passing the green, turn left to continue into the town centre.

Turn right on to the A6071, which descends to the riverside and crosses over a narrow bridge controlled by traffic lights. Shortly afterwards turn right and ascend to the village of Walton.

At the junction beyond Walton turn left on to the B6318. The road gains height gradually, although with dips into small valleys, and passes the hamlets of Kirkcambeck and Lyneholmeford. At Lyneholmeford cross the White Lyne river and take the next right, signed for Bewcastle, about 1km (³/₄ mile) further on.

This road drops down steadily then regains height before a final drop to the White Lyne valley. Once over the river, follow the road above Kirk Beck to the village of Bewcastle. The road is marked with wooden posts into the village.

For the cross and the exhibition about Bewcastle's long history, turn left on the road indicated 'Bewcastle Cross'; this leads up to the church.

Leave Bewcastle by returning to the same road, continuing through the hamlet and crossing the stream. Follow the road for about 8km (5 miles) until it ends at a crossroads. Go straight ahead, crossing a valley, and continue on this road as it drops down into the Irthing Valley and bends right to follow the river towards Lanercost Priory.

From Lanercost Priory follow the road over the river, heading towards Brampton. Continue

Above: A view towards the Scottish border from above Bewcastle.

along this lane as it ascends steadily then loses height coming into Brampton. At the junction turn right into Brampton, then take the next left into the town square. Turn left on to the B6413. Follow this road out of Brampton, crossing over the A69 bypass with care. After 1¹/₂ km (1 mile) turn left for Brampton station. The lane follows the railway, taking you to the Carlisle-bound platform of the station.

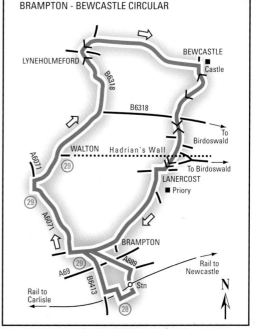

ROUTE 30
BEYOND THE WALL INTO BORDER COUNTRY: BRAMPTON - BEWCASTLE CIRCULAR

The Cumbria Cycleway
(417km [259 miles])
This is a circular route round the edge of the county (which at the time of going to press is subject to major revisions). From Carlisle it goes up the Eden Valley, through the edge of the Yorkshire Dales, down the Lune Valley, around the edge of Morecambe Bay to the Furness peninsula and follows the west coast around to the Solway Firth.

C2C Whitehaven to Sunderland
(225km [140 miles])
This challenging route, much of it off-road, uses an old railway trackbed to make a gradual climb out of the old port of Whitehaven before heading eastwards into the Cumbrian fells. The route then crosses the northern part of the Lake District on its way east through Penrith and the high passes of the North Pennines. Route 19 uses the separate bike path for the descent into Whitehaven.

The Reivers Cycle Route
(301km [187 miles])
Tynemouth to Whitehaven via Kielder, the Scottish borders and Carlisle. Further information can be obtained from Sustrans (see p.111).

Hadrian's Wall Cycle Route
(NCN 72)
This is a new cycle route currently being developed to follow the line of Hadrian's Wall World Heritage Site from the Solway Firth to Tynemouth. It follows the Cumbria Cycleway between Silloth and Brampton. Route 26 in this book uses part of the route along the Solway coast.

The Lancashire Cycleway
(402km [250 miles])
Several routes in this book use sections of the Lancashire Cycleway. The cycleway was originally two circular routes in the north and south of the county. Both are now joined at Whalley. The southern route runs through the West Lancashire Plain round Ormskirk and through the West Pennine moors into the East Lancashire district of Pendle and the West Pennines themselves. The northern route runs through the Fylde Plain, over the limestone hills of Silverdale by Morecambe Bay and through the Forest of Bowland moors to the Ribble Valley. A guide booklet to the Lancashire Cycleway is available from Lancashire County Council (details below).

Preston & South Ribble
A network of routes linked to the Lancashire cycleway has been developed by the local authority; telephone 01772 264609 for a leaflet.

Trans-Pennine Trail
(329 km [205 miles])
The Trans-Pennine Trail runs from Southport to Hull and Hornsea across the Pennines via Merseyside, Greater Manchester and South and West Yorkshire almost entirely on off-road cycle routes or very quiet, traffic-free lanes. Route 2 uses a section of the trail on leaving Southport. Full details of the whole route and sections in the northwest are available from the TPT Officer, Barnsley Council Planning Services, Central Offices, Kendray Street, Barnsley, S70 2TN (tel: 01226 772567).

National Cycle Route 6
Preston to Lancaster
National Cycle Route 7
Glasgow–Carlisle–Penrith
Sections of both these waymarked NC routes are used in this guide. Full details and maps can be obtained direct from Sustrans (details p.111).

Right: Medieval bridleway near Samlesbury Bottoms

CUMBRIA COUNTY COUNCIL
Citadel Chambers
Carlisle CA3 8SG
Tel: 01228 812812 (Travelink)
Website: www.cumbria.gov.uk

CARLISLE VISITOR CENTRE
Old Town Hall
Carlisle, Cumbria CA3 8JH
Tel: 01228 625600

CUMBRIA TOURIST BOARD
Ashleigh
Holly Road, Windermere
Cumbria LA23 2AQ
Tel: 015394 44444
Website: www.gocumbria.co.uk

Tourist information in Cumbria is linked to
public transport information through the
British Tourist Authority website:
www.visitbritain.com.

**LAKE DISTRICT NATIONAL
PARK AUTHORITY**
Murley Moss
Oxenholme Road, Kendal
Cumbria LA9 7RL
Tel: 01539 724555
Website: www.lake-district.gov.uk

LANCASHIRE COUNTY COUNCIL
The County Public Relations Officer
PO Box 78, County Hall
Preston PR1 8XJ
Tel: 01772 263521

NORTHWEST TOURIST BOARD
Swan House
Swan Meadow, Wigan
Lancashire WN3 5BB
Tel: 01942 821222
Website: www.visitbritain.com/
north-west-England

Below: Terrace Gardens, Lever Park, Rivington

CYCLING PROJECT FOR THE NORTH WEST

A charity which promotes cycling for all in the northwest of England, including those with disabilities. The Cycling Project for the North West also provides a national information and advisory service on cycling matters to the public as well as to local authorities and companies.

1 Enterprise Park
Agecroft Road
Pendlebury
Manchester
M27 8WA
Tel: 0161 745 9099/9088
email: cpnw@cycling.org.uk
Website: www.cycling.org.uk

CYCLISTS' TOURING CLUB (CTC)

The UK National Body campaigning for cycling in both town and countryside.

69 Meadrow
Godalming, Surrey GU7 3HS
Tel: 01483 417217
Website: www.ctc.org.uk

SUSTRANS

Sustrans — the name stands for 'Sustainable Transport' — is a national charity which works locally and nationally to build new traffic-free cycleways, operating as both an engineering company and a campaigning body. Sustrans is currently developing and promoting the 8,000km (5,000-mile) UK National Cycle Network.

Information on the National Cycle Network, plus a range of cycling publications and maps for the UK can be obtained direct from Sustrans:

35 King Street
Bristol BS1 4DZ
Tel: 0117 929 0888
email: info@nationalcyclenetwork.org.uk
Website: www.nationalcyclenetwork.org.uk

BIKE RAIL

This DETR/Countryside Agency-sponsored consultancy deals with the specific issue of provision of cycle space at railway stations and the carriage of cycles on trains.

3 Pottery Street, London SE16 4PH
Tel: 020 7252 3696

Above: Cyclists near Ainsdale

COUNTRYGOER

A national campaign based on a website promoting sustainable travel (walking, cycling and public transport) to and through the UK national parks and the countryside, with links to Europe.

Website: www.countrygoer.org

OTHER USEFUL CYCLING GUIDEBOOKS

Byway Biking in Lancashire
Henry Tindell (Sigma Press)
Twenty-seven mainly off-road routes within Lancashire.

Cycling in Cumbria & the Lake District
Mike Hutchinson and Neil Wheadon (Collins)
A wide variety of mostly on-road routes, with 25 fully mapped cycle tours.

Wilde's Cycle Route Guide to Lancashire & the Lake District
Gillian Rowan-Wilde (Gildersleve)
Nineteen rides on- and off-road.

Cycling without Traffic: The North
Colin & Lydia Speakman (Dial House)
A guide to traffic-free cycling in the north of England, including many cyclepaths.

CycleCity Guide Manchester
A useful map for Mancunians wishing to find a route to the nearest railway station to travel to Lancashire or Cumbria.

Bowland by Bike
Eleven rides through Bowland with route information and places of interest.